Joy Shtick

or What Is the Existential Vacuum and Does It Come with Attachments?

Joy Shtick

❀ or What Is the
Existential Vacuum
and Does It Come
with Attachments?

Joy Behar

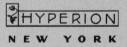

HYPERION

NEW YORK

LIBRARY OF CONGRESS CATALOGING-IN-PUBLICATION DATA

Behar, Joy.
Joy shtick, or what is the existential vacuum and does it come with attachments? / by Joy Behar. — 1st ed.
p. cm.
ISBN 0-7868-6423-0
I. Title
PN6162.B3736   1999
792.7'028'092—dc21   98-42761
                                    CIP

FIRST EDITION

10 9 8 7 6 5 4 3 2 1

Book Design by Lovedog Studio

**For Steve and Eve,
who keep me laughing.**

Acknowledgments

I'd like to thank the following people:

Charles Salzberg for his contributions and for helping me to coordinate this book and focus me on the task. Thank God his memory is intact. Also, for allowing my dog Max to hump his leg during our meetings.

My editor, Gretchen Young. She and her baby Greer were a constant source of encouragement. She actively participated in the process and for that I am grateful.

Steve Janowitz for his continued support, creativity, and affection. He is what a boyfriend is supposed to be.

Jane Bowling . . . the stuff we wrote in the old days is still funny.

Larry Amos, the quickest wit in the east.

And Andrew Smith, for helping me to be funny every day.

Also the following people for their support, their friendship, and the endless amount of time we've spent on the phone discussing the vicissitudes of life which helped fill up this book: Susie Essman, Taffy Manuelian, Suzy Soro, Leslie Ayvasian, John Bacher, Kaye Ballard, Madeline Sollaccio, Marilyn Raisen, and especially Angela Maggio (aka Sissy).

For giving me a forum over the years and for their supportive friendship: Caroline Hirsch, Rick Newman, Cary and Suzanne Hoffman, Sam Schact, Richard Fields. Squire Rushnell, Leah Sutton, Paul Herzick, Burt Levitt, Susan Engel, Fred Weinhaus, Mitch Gallob, Jamie DeRoy, Angela La-Greca, Arnold Graham, Howie Rapp, Hank Gallo, David Rothenberg, and, of course, Louis Farranda, who has provided all of the above, plus many laughs.

Grazie to my sorelli at the National Organization of Italian American Women, particularly Donna De Matteo, Aileen Sirey, and Pat Misasi.

My friends at the Friars Club, including Jean Pierre Trebot, Freddie Roman, Frank Capitelli, Joy Golden, Laura Slutsky, Ruth Stern, and Jack L. Greene.

Cyrena Esposito, the most enthusiastic and supportive agent I've ever met.

All my friends at "The View": Bill Geddie, Star Jones, Meredith Vieira, Debbie Metanopolous, Fran Taylor, Julie Alderfer, Julie Siegel, Dusty Cohen, Jessica Steadman Guff, Linda Finson, Dom Nuzzi, Mark Gentile, Kelly Vahey, Nina Silvestri, Hank Norman, Mark Lipinsky, Beverly Kopf, Sue Podbielski, Allison Kluger, Rebecca Biderman, Julie

Cooper, Erin Saxton, Anne-Marie Williams Gray, Jakki Taylor, Alicia Ybarbo, Augie Jakovac, Karith Foster, Evelien Kong, Jeanne Sullivan, Matt Strauss, Matt Wright, Richard Polonetsky, Dana Goodman, Julie Cooper, Donald Berman, and Sue Solomon. Also the magicians with brushes and lipsticks: Marque, Diedre Flaherty, Eve Pearl, and Alan Cutler. (Did I forget anybody?)

The Network, for their support, friendship, and power lunches: Angela Shapiro, Pat Fili-Krushel, Valerie Schaer, and Holly Jacobs.

A very special thank you to Barbara Walters who gave me a job on network television and didn't think I was "too New York" for the rest of America.

To my family, who gave me the freedom to express myself in a way that was not always polite. First and foremost, to my aunt Julie Carbone and my uncle Dickie Carbone. Also Paula Kleban who escorted me to my first audition in Junior High School (I didn't get the part, but thanks anyway).

To my darling, special, beautiful daughter, Eve Behar. Thanks for being perfect. And to her father, Joseph Behar, for helping to produce her.

Most of all, I owe a great debt of gratitude and a lot of funny material to my departed relatives, especially my mother, Rose Occhiuto, my father Louis (Gino) Occhiuto, aunt Sadie Carbone, and Rose and Joe Caruso. (I hope they're all laughing in Heaven at the jokes about them.)

Contents

1. **Trapped at Exit 60**   1

2. **My Life in Funeral Parlors**   13

3. **RANDOM THOUGHT**
    Drugs   23

4. **Why I Hate the Beach**   25

5. **A Near-Death Experience That**
    Saved My Life   31

6. **RANDOM THOUGHT**
    The Promise Keepers   49

7. **Don't Ask Joy . . .**
    Unless You Want the Real Answer   51

8. **Women Over Fifty**
    Have It All Together,
    But Everything Is Falling Apart   55

9. **Don't Ask Joy . . .**
    Unless You Want the Real Answer   67

10. **RANDOM THOUGHT**
    Pornography   71

11. Eight Minutes of Terror 73

12. Joy's Travelogue—
    Picnics in the Cemetery 81

13. Watch (What You Say) on the Rhine 87

14. Going Down on a Mule 91

15. You Can't Count on Monte Cristo 93

16. California Screaming 97

17. RANDOM THOUGHT
    Hollywood 99

18. Chestnuts Roasting
    on an Open Friar 101

19. RANDOM THOUGHT
    Eating Disorders 111

20. Don't Ask Joy . . .
    Unless You Want the Real Answer 113

21. Dogs I Have Known—
    A Photo Essay 117

22. RANDOM THOUGHT
    Learning Disabilities 121

23. Marriage and Other Gambles 123

24. RANDOM THOUGHT
    Living Wills 133

25. Leni Riefenstahl—
    An Imaginary Interview 135

26. **Celebrity Sucking Up**   139

27. **The Wrong Century to Be
    a Woman**   145

28. *Je Ne Regrette Rien*   153

29. **RANDOM THOUGHT
    St. Patrick's Day Parade**   161

30. **Some Thoughts On the
    History of Birth Control,
    or PMS Flashbacks**   163

31. **RANDOM THOUGHT
    Give the DNA a Chance to Breathe**   169

32. **Camille and Gloria**   171

33. **RANDOM THOUGHT
    Doctors and Their Big Mouths**   177

34. **The Incredible, Absolutely
    True Story of Lorena and John**   179

35. **Sadie's News and Advice
    from the Neighborhood**   183

36. **How to Tell If You're Really Italian:
    The True and False Test**   189

37. **RANDOM THOUGHT
    The Miranda Rights**   191

Dear Sirs:

  This past Thursday, Joy Behar was once again bashing Pat Robertson on the air. This deranged excuse for a woman seems to have a personal vendetta against this poor man. I personally have alerted the Christian Coalition, the American Center for Law and Justice, and Pat Robertson about Joy Behar. I've sent them tapes of her venomous ravings, so be warned. Your station is too good for a demonic twit like her to be on. There are hundreds of good comics in New York. Please consider cleaning up the airwaves by replacing that insidious gutter-snipe.

  I won't sign my name because I fear retaliation from Behar. I honestly believe she's an evil being. Dump her . . . the sooner the better.

Sincerely,

A Listener

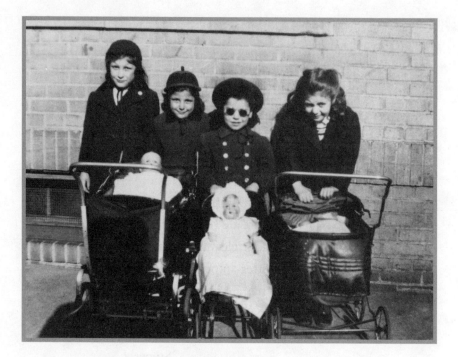

Portrait of the artist as
a demonic twit.

Dear Listener:

In the name of Geraldo Rivera and all Satanic cults, may I wish you baldness and impotence that even Viagra will not cure.

Fondly,

Joy

Insidious gutter-snipe or bowling
champ? You decide.

Trapped at Exit 60

Twenty-five years ago I lived way out on Long Island, off Exit 60 on the infamous Long Island Expressway, in what could best be described as a below-working-class neighborhood. My immediate neighbors were living in a shack. An interesting circumstance, since Exit 70, en route to the Hamptons, held the promise of bumping into Ali MacGraw or Alan Alda.

People did not smile much in my neighborhood. At first I thought they were unhappy, and then I realized that it was probably because everyone seemed to have teeth missing. Apparently, dentistry stopped at Exit 59.

I might as well have been living on a cattle ranch in Montana. I was totally isolated from civilization, but without the nice scenery. I had very few friends in the area. None of my neighbors spoke to me. But how could they? They never saw me. I rarely left the house. I spent most of my time at home rereading *In Cold Blood.* That Truman Capote really had a special knack for making lonely shut-ins feel secure.

I was married at the time and my daughter was coming up on a year old. My husband was earning his doctorate in Sociology at the State University at Stony Brook, which explained why we were living at the edge of the earth. He and his fellow graduate students dreamed of writing treatises on such fascinating topics as "the latent function of social interaction and conflictual reality of subcultures as defined by the liberating potential of subjective interpretation and Berna Skrypnek." While he slaved away over a hot typewriter, obsessed with topics that would only be read by other sociologists who were busily writing their own scintillating essays, I was desperately trying to figure out how to wean my daughter off my breast, which she was beginning to chomp on like she was some kind of wild marsupial.

Immediately after my daughter was born, I threw myself into a creative, domestic frenzy. Apparently, giving birth had triggered in me a long dormant urge to express myself artistically. I took a watercolor class; I began to write short stories; but it was puppetry that was my real poison. Once I got started I couldn't stop myself from making papier-mâché puppets that bore a striking resemblance to my relatives back in Brooklyn. The puppet I made of my Aunt Rose was not only anatomically correct, but it even sported a mink stole. I might have been prescient, because I didn't realize that some form of occupational therapy, even if it involved making family archetypes, would later be needed to rouse me out of my postpartum depression.

When I wasn't fashioning puppets, I was working on a master's degree in English Education and writing papers about Flannery O'Connor. In the meantime, all my plants were blooming as if they had been blessed with some potent fertilizer from another planet. It was as if Martha Stewart, Mrs. Greenthumbs, and Shari Lewis were channeling through me.

Life was good. At least for the moment. But one day all that changed. Without warning, and for no apparent physical reason, I awoke one morning and could not get out of bed. It felt as if someone had stapled me to my mattress. Try as I might, I just couldn't get up.

Suddenly, all of my projects seemed irrelevant and stupid. The puppets in particular seemed like a total waste of time. Who would ever care about these stupid puppets? Even my relatives, whom they were fashioned after, would be bored by them, or so I figured.

If it weren't for my daughter screaming for my boob, I would have been happy to lie there indefinitely. This lethargy went on for about six months. But as I lay there, staring at the ceiling, my husband slowly—very slowly—began to notice. Apparently his treatise on the distribution of paper clips in corporate America was finally completed and he had time to check on me.

After a while, when it seemed as if I might be stapled to that mattress indefinitely, I finally realized that I couldn't spend the rest of my life like this and so I roused myself enough to call a shrink and try to make an appointment.

The only other experience I had had with therapy was right after I was married. I was searching for a creative outlet to enrich my life and this shrink suggested that I have a baby. Amazingly, despite this earlier dubious brush with psychotherapy, I still decided to go back a second time. Maybe it was because Exit 60 was such a lonely place that I was even willing to pay for what I figured would be good conversation.

This therapist came highly recommended, and was actually described to me as "a shot of vitamin B-12," which, under the circumstances, didn't sound too bad, especially since there would be no sharp instruments involved. Unfortunately, the therapist said she was "very busy right now," and so I would have to wait a couple of months to see her. This was unsatisfactory, as I was already creating an indentation in the mattress that was making it almost impossible to extricate myself, even if I had wanted to. So I informed her that I had to see her immediately because I was trapped "under the bell jar." Those of you who have had periods of depression of some sort or another will certainly recall that the patron saint of dreariness, Sylvia Plath, had written a book called *The Bell Jar* a short time before she put her head into her oven while her kids were sleeping. (Why wake them? It was hard enough getting them to sleep.)

Fortunately, this shrink, who was evidently familiar with the book, grasped the gravity of my situation and so she cleared out her busy calendar and made an appointment with me immediately. This taught me an important lesson: when choosing a therapist, find one who is more familiar with poetry than with the latest Spice Girls hit.

The shrink was a woman of about fifty, with a limp left over from childhood polio. To this day, I maintain that she was my favorite therapist because not only did she spend more than the allotted time with me, but she once offered me a piece of cheese when I had low blood sugar, making it impossible to sufficiently concentrate on my neurosis. Most therapists will let you lie there like a dog before they'll offer you any food or even some candy. I'm sure they have some sort of explanation for this, like "Feeding patients will just trigger a stronger transferential environment." Yeah, right. Advice to therapists who might be reading this: it wouldn't kill you to have a bowl of M&Ms next to the couch.

For several months, I met with my new shrink once a week and we discussed my childhood experiences. A typical session might go something like this:

Shrink: Tell me about your childhood.

Joy: I never got a lot of sleep.

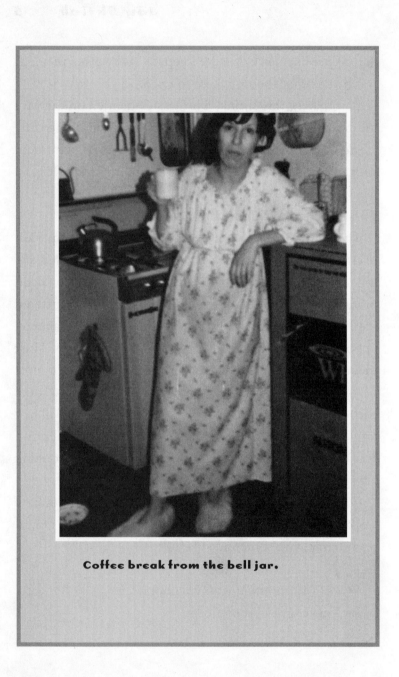

Coffee break from the bell jar.

Shrink: Why? Were you having nightmares?

Joy: No. I was the TV set. My relatives kept me awake to entertain them. How many times can you sing "On the Good Ship Lollipop" and still make it fresh?

Shrink: Is that why you spend so much time in bed now?

Joy: How the hell do I know?

Shrink: Why are you getting hostile? What's troubling you?

Joy: I hate Long Island.

Shrink: Why? It's so lovely here. Have you visited the new outlet center?

Joy: I shoplifted . . . I mean, I shopped, there. I know it well.

Shrink: A Freudian slip.

Joy: No, actually just a cute top.

Shrink: You mean to tell me if you weren't out here on Long Island that your problems would be solved?

Joy: I need to see human beings.

Shrink: Why don't you get out of bed and go somewhere.

Joy: Where?

Shrink: That's up to you. Where would you like to go?

Joy: Back to the tenement.

Shrink: Why?

Joy: I like the smell of garbage at night. Which reminds me. The cheese you gave me smells like my father's socks.

Shrink: It seems that we've struck a psychosexual chord here.

Joy: We have?

Shrink: I believe there is a strong parallel between your inability to extricate yourself from your bed and the smell of your father's socks. Have you had any interesting dreams lately?

Joy: Last night I dreamed that I was eighty years old and I was reading from the Bible at a senior citizens' center. Just as I was getting to the best part, my brassiere went flying into somebody's soup.

Shrink: What do you mean by the best part?

Joy: When they talk about turning that guy's wife into a pillar of salt.

Shrink: Lot's wife. His name is Lot. What does that remind you of?

Joy: I don't know.

Shrink: Think hard.

Joy: Well. Maybe it's about my life. That I'm like a woman frozen in salt. And that I feel like I'll be an old lady before I ever do what I want to do. Is that what you mean?

Shrink: Not really. Brassiere? Soup? Salt? What do they all have in common?

Joy: They all come in cups?

Shrink: Now you got it.

Eventually, after weeks of conversations like this, she said to me, "You don't need a shrink. You need a drama school." And so she recommended I go to one in Huntington, Long Island. Practical guidance from a shrink? Unheard of. Would Freud have suggested obedience school to the Wolfman? Another helpful note for you therapists out there: remember, the world does not end at your couch, and fifty minutes is not an hour.

It was at this drama school that I met an acting teacher named Zena, who was a product of the old studio days in Hollywood. Her best friends were Jose Ferrer ("I will never forgive Joe Ferrer for playing Richard the third like a cripple," she often bemoaned) and Susan Hayward, who had just died of a brain tumor. Apparently Miss Hayward had the misfortune of once being cast in a movie that was shooting in the middle of a desert where they were testing A-bombs. Everyone on that film, including John Wayne who thought he "beat the big C," has died. And I don't think the film did too well, either.

Zena was the kind of teacher who believed that telling is teaching. We rarely got a chance to act because she was all too happy to do it for us. She would say that we were going to learn "insanity" and then she would do "insanity." Her technique was strictly "snake pit." She'd say, in a normal voice, "I really love roses," and then she'd change her voice or put her hands up as if she were carrying a tray of canapes, and say it again, "I really love roses," her face distorted, teeth bared, and looking more like a hemorrhoid sufferer than a schizophrenic.

Even though I never got a chance to act much, I really liked that class. That's because Zena always said that I was talented. I'm not sure how she knew that, but it was nice to hear anyway. Frankly, that's really all it takes for me to like something. I need to be good at it, or at least told that I'm good at it. It's as simple as that. For that reason, Zena was a *great* acting teacher.

Despite Zena's teaching methods, I finally got a chance to do a scene in class. I didn't know much about acting technique, so I bought an LP of Uta Hagen as Martha in *Who's Afraid of Virginia Woolf?* and I copied the way she did it. "That was brilliant," Zena announced to my fellow drama students. "Notice the way Joy owned the stage. She's an actress!" Suddenly, Zena was a genius in my eyes.

You'd think this positive reinforcement would have encouraged me to join the Actors Studio, or at least to call Uta Hagen and thank her, wouldn't you? But, even though Zena loved my work and the shrink continued to feed me emotionally not to mention with cheese, I still couldn't see my way out of Exit 60 and into a new life.

But things were looking up. At least I was functioning on a more normal plane. For one thing, I was vertical. And for another, the kid was off the boob and my husband was finishing up his doctoral thesis.

One day I woke up in a cold sweat and, without thinking, I boldly announced to my husband that we were going to sell the house and move back to civilization. He was stunned by this sudden outburst (after all, he was used to me just lying there) but he agreed without much fuss. (Maybe the fact that I looked like Linda Blair in *The Exorcist* at that moment helped convince him.) At any rate, he knew that he could discuss "the collective behavior and anticipatory socialization of the Lemon Swamp" within the confines of the five boroughs just as easily as he could on the periphery of humanity known as the suburbs. Anyway, we both knew that we didn't want our daughter to grow up to live in a trailer park and marry a guy covered with tattoos.

In my heart, I always knew I was going to leave Exit 60, go to Uta Hagen's class, visit my real relatives instead of making facsimiles, continue therapy, pick up a copy of Jacqueline Susann's latest trash novel, and find a good dentist. Turns out, that was a very good plan for me.

You'll have to read my ex-husband's latest treatise to find out how it worked for him.

My Life in
Funeral Parlors

Not long ago, I attended the wake of a long-time acquaintance of mine. The deceased had two daughters and one of them was grieving openly, bemoaning the fact that she no longer had a mother. Her aunt, a woman of limited resources, was doing her own brand of grieving, trying out her theory of lost relativity while at the same time ostensibly trying to comfort her niece.

"Yes," she said, "you lost a mother, but I lost a sister. And Nana lost a daughter. And your father lost a wife. And your son lost a grandmother. And Carmine Pecoraro lost a friend." The list went on for what seemed like forever. And the building lost a tenant. And the dentist lost a patient. And the butcher lost a meat lover. Finally, I lost interest and, needless to say, the poor girl was not consoled.

For me, and certainly James Joyce, and now apparently

TV programmers, wakes have an odd, almost surreal attraction. From the Princess Diana funeral to the Sonny Bono funeral, there seems to be a tremendous interest in funerals. Italian funerals have yet to be televised. Maybe it's because with so many women throwing themselves into the grave, it's hard to tell who the deceased is. But Italian wakes are incredibly interesting. Where else do you get a horseshoe of gardenias saying SUCCESS except when an Italian dies.

As a child, I was brought to many wakes in my old neighborhood in Brooklyn. It was almost like going to a birthday party, what with me decked out in my Shirley Temple pinafores. On the other hand, most of the other people who attended these wakes wore black or some other subdued color to show respect. But not everyone. I remember one woman who walked into the funeral parlor where the body was laid out, wearing a red outfit with shoes to match and a hat with feathers. Everyone was stopped cold in their tracks, or as my mother's friend Mary Ricciardi used to say, "We remained." They just "remained" in their horrified state, shocked at the temerity, the audacity, the utter tackiness of the outfit. Or how can I forget Carmine Russo, who shocked my family when he sauntered into my grandmother's wake wearing a T-shirt and displaying a tattoo of the Last Supper. My Aunt Sadie simply remarked that she had no idea that Carmine was that religious.

Initially, these wakes, often given for people who were strangers as far as I was concerned, were kind of scary for me.

After the wake, dad picks his teeth.

But as I grew older, they would prove to be a wonderful source of fun. They also provided an unexpected method of altering my mother's mood, which most often matched the predominant color worn at these gatherings: black. On any given day, I'd be likely to find her at the sink listening to a recording of *La Traviata*, streams of tears rolling down her cheeks, relentlessly reliving all the depressing moments of her life. The only way you could cheer her up was to inform her that you were going to a wake. "Oh, yeah?" she'd say, her voice rising gleefully. "Who died?" And suddenly the blood would rush back to her face. Once again, life was worth living.

My Aunt Sadie was another frequent wake attendee. In fact, over the years she attended so many wakes that she should have received frequent flyer mileage. Aunt Sadie didn't have to actually know the deceased. If she passed them on the street once or twice on her way to the sausage store, that was enough of a relationship for her. After all, wakes were often social situations where you ran into old friends and neighbors. If the person in the coffin was old, there usually was a lot of talking, smoking, and general shmoozing in the antechamber. And Aunt Sadie could talk, smoke, and shmooze with the best of them. That there happened to be a dead body in the room seemed at best an ornament, and at worst, irrelevant. Nor did it put a damper on the occasion.

Oh, yes. The deceased. To some an afterthought, but after all, if it weren't for the dear departed, my mother would

After the wake, dad takes a nap.

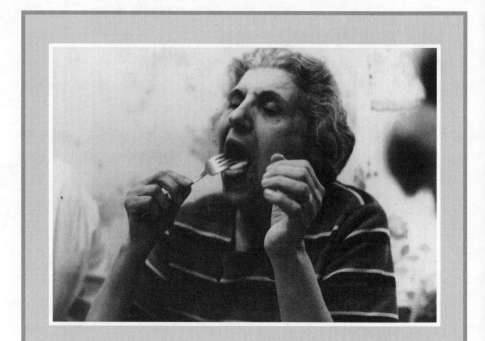

After the wake, Aunt Rose has a snack.

be sobbing at the sink listening to Italian operas and Aunt Sadie would be talking to herself.

To me, one of the more bizarre traditions coming out of religion is the Christian custom of putting makeup on dead people, dressing them in fancy outfits, and fixing their hair in some sort of coif, all of which inevitably prompts various people to make comments like, "He looks good." Or, "He looks just like himself." (Who else would he look like?—all he got was an embalming, not plastic surgery.) Rarely, however, do you hear, "He never looked better," although in some cases I have seen, this would be a far more accurate observation.

My Aunt Rose often got into trouble at wakes because her voice carried and she was quite capable of making an inappropriate comment that would be heard across the room. Once, a woman she knew from childhood accused her of making fun of her dentures. My aunt claimed that she was not talking about the woman's teeth, but an argument broke out anyway.

Denture Woman: Are you laughing at my teeth?

Aunt Rose: What are you, crazy?

Denture Woman: I saw you. You were staring at my mouth and then you said something to your sister-in-law and then you both laughed.

Aunt Rose: I was not laughing at your teeth. I was laughing at Carmela Mangiapropette. She had toilet paper on her shoe.

Denture Woman: Don't lie, Rose. I know how vicious
you can be.

Aunt Rose: Me? And what about you? I heard you call
your daughter-in-law a *putana*.

Denture Woman: That's a lie. I never called her a *putana*,
even if she was one. And what about that time when
you put soap in your mother-in-law's mouth?

Aunt Rose: She deserved it. She was cursing me up and
down.

Denture Woman: You're a bitch and you know it.

Aunt Rose: And you're a buck-toothed old hag. I don't
think it's a laughing matter when someone pays
thousands of dollars on dentures and ends up looking like she's running at Aqueduct.

When my mother died, people were pretty upset. She was
one of those people who never made an enemy. She was in-
capable of hurting anyone's feelings. She never said a mean
word to me, or anyone else for that matter. All in all, she was
a good mother, despite the occasional fits of melancholia,
which she couldn't help. If it were today, she'd be on Prozac
and my life would have been a picnic. I don't know if I would
have become a comedian, however, since the motivation to
save the world from its misery would be missing.

One of my friends, a comedian who has a hideous relationship with his mother, came to my mother's wake to pay
his respects. Comedians are a rare breed. First of all, they

After the wake, Aunt Julie has a
few choice words for the living.

have trouble with serious situations, and secondly, they say whatever they want, God bless them. So there we were standing in the smoking room with a few people, and suddenly he says to me, "Joy, you are so lucky. You have a boyfriend, you have a career, and now you have a dead mother."

Believe it or not, we had a good laugh over that. My mother would have laughed, too.

Random Thought

Drugs

I'm not into drugs. Never have been. Maybe it's because doing drugs is often about sharing things—like joints and cocaine. I'm an only child. I don't share.

Marijuana, now there's a brilliant drug. Just what I need. Something to stimulate my appetite.

I'm against legalizing drugs, because it would only bring the stuff closer to home and make everyone think it's okay to use it. I imagine my Uncle Dom walking in the door. "Hey, I picked up some crack to go with the lasagne. I'm just gonna sprinkle some of this angel dust in with the pesto, okay Rosie?" Next thing you know, Julia Child would be lacing the boeuf bourguignon with smack.

There is, however, one drug I never refuse: novo-caine. Can you imagine what a nightmare it must have been before they invented painkillers? What did they use, a bottle of whiskey? Or have a guy bite a bullet? That's an anesthetic? They could have done a lot better than that. How about bringing in a big-breasted woman? That would distract any man. You could stick a knife through their arm, they see those big breasts, they don't feel a thing.

For women, why not try a fashion show? Just do the surgery on a runway with those models parading by, wearing the new fall line, and I guarantee you could do a cesarean on most women and they wouldn't even notice.

Why I Hate the Beach

Last summer, I decided to rent a house at the beach for the month of July. Not August. Just July. I don't like the beach enough to rent for July and August. In fact, I don't really like the beach at all.

For one thing, I only like sand if it's really flat. Which is probably why I prefer cement, which is flat, unless you're living in New York City, the pothole capital of the world. Cement doesn't move, and it doesn't get into your bathing suit, unless you owe money to the wrong people.

Things always seem to go wrong at the beach. For instance, a lot of people I know love the beach and sit there for hours, their faces aimed religiously toward the sun, as if it's somehow going to change their lives. And it does. After years of staring toward the sun, they now need face-lifts, laser surgery, and eye jobs. Is this, I wonder, an acceptable price for sitting in the sand?

25

Watering the Chia pet.

Besides, my hair has a weird reaction to the beach, a reaction that makes me anxious. My hair is naturally very, very curly, even in winter, and on the beach it just takes off and grows like one of those Chia pets, eventually going completely out of control. This is unacceptable, because as with many women, my hair is a very important asset, especially on the head.

When I was a kid, I used to go to the local hairdresser armed with pictures of Carol Lynley. I'd hold up the picture, smile demurely, and ask the hairdresser if she could do my hair like Carol's. I must have been in a psychotic episode since Carol Lynley had long, blonde, *straight* hair, while mine was dark and curly. And the hairdresser I was trying to offer guidance to was tough. Her name was Rocco. Her vocabulary consisted of three words: friggin', pisser, and balls, and sometimes she could work them all into the same sentence. But I was adamant. I insisted on the Carol Lynley hairstyle. When Rocco would finally stop laughing and start to work on me, she'd wind up doing something to my hair that made me look more like a founding father or a deranged eighteenth-century composer than a grade-B movie actress. I'd run home crying and soak my head in water, which kind of defeated the purpose of the whole salon experience.

I'd like to learn to like the beach. I really would. It seems like a pretty easy way to spend the summer. People claim to forget their troubles when they're there. They read, they swim, they run, they listen to the radio, they walk around without shoes, socks, and pantyhose. But when you think about it, except for the swimming, I can do all those things in the privacy and comfort of my own house.

To some, the beach is a mystical experience. I remember once reading a poem by Anne Sexton where she wrote that lying in the sun was like having intercourse with God. A sex survey I read said that women most likely to have an orgasm every time are conservative Protestants. Isn't that something? What does this say about progressive women? Are we so preoccupied with change that we can't take the time to enjoy a little nookie? Have these conservative women been keeping something from us? Is Newt Gingrich more than an annoying gnome with bad politics? Is Rush Limbaugh a great lay? Maybe it's because these women have more money and so they're better able to relax. After all, I suppose there's nothing like a solid Keogh plan to put a girl at ease.

But this notion of having sex with God on the beach is very tempting because, frankly, I could use the orgasm. And besides, it would be nice to yell out the name of the person I'm actually having sex with for a change. This is probably something that could get me to the beach, for July and August.

In the past, though, every time I've gone to the beach I've wound up irritated, not satiated. Maybe it's me. Maybe I'm frigid. I mean, if you can't get off with the most omnipotent of all beings, it seems to me you might have a problem. Maybe I was too self-conscious. Maybe it was because I felt

The tenement version of Waikiki beach,
also known as the roof.

fat in my bathing suit. Or maybe I didn't think God would find me attractive. After all, I was taught that God is very judgmental. He decides who goes where after death. Maybe I thought that He'd be too critical and that He'd judge me too fat to have sex with. I can imagine myself lying on the beach in anticipation of the big O and God is having a ménage à trois with two teenage girls on the next blanket.

Another reason I hate the beach is that I can't sit still. I remember that when I was ten, my parents took me to Asbury Park, New Jersey, for vacation. It was the only vacation they ever took me on, unless you count our family picnics in the cemetery. I didn't like Asbury Park. I was fidgety. I couldn't sit still. Even then, I didn't see the point of it. The beach, I mean. About midway through our vacation to the beach, my father decided he had cancer. Of course, he didn't actually have cancer, but he was convinced he did. I still don't know what put that in his head, but as I recall, most of the vacation was spent on the beach with him staring into space. Or sitting in the motel room with him staring at the wall while my mother dusted. After the week was up, my parents sent me to Springfield, Mass., to stay with my cousin Tonia. When I came back, my father didn't think he had cancer anymore. School started and everything went back to normal. But I never went back to Asbury Park.

This summer, I think I'll try to enjoy the beach. But just for July, just in case God decides to throw me a quick one.

A Near-Death Experience That Saved My Life

It was 1979, and I was attending the funeral of my friend Arthur. Poor Arthur had dropped dead of a heart attack. One day he was with us, the next day he was gone. Just like that.

Arthur was a rarity, a dyed-in-the-wool Marxist except that he had a pretty good sense of humor, which actually made him something of an unusual Marxist. Even better, he laughed at my stuff, which made me like him more than most of the other Marxists I happened to know. Arthur, a true believer, had opened a place he called The School for a Marxist Education, where, among other things, he would put together seminars and all kinds of other events just to get people in the door so he could make converts out of them. Since cakes and cookies were served most people came to nosh, not to learn about Marxism. Arthur convinced me and some of my friends to put on shows for his school. Since I was relatively new at performing and figured I could use the experience, I accepted and, along with Taffy Jaffe, Jeffrey Essman, Charles Barnet, and Bernard Lias, we agreed to come up with some entertainment for budding Marxists. We had free rein. Bernard would get into drag and sing a Supremes hit. We'd mock all the politicians, right and left. We weren't very polished, but they loved us anyway. Come to think of it, maybe it was because, like the cakes and cookies, we didn't cost anything. Or maybe it was our unabashed irreverence that appealed to them.

Those folks were the best audience I ever had, and they spoiled me. I'd go to a comedy club, do the same material, and I'd bomb. But at The School for a Marxist Education I was always a hit; so I owed a lot to Arthur and his school. Which explains why I was at his funeral in Greenwich Village.

So there I was, standing in the back of the church, listening to the eulogies, and the next thing I knew I was lying on the floor, with this excruciating pain in my abdomen, shooting all the way up my shoulders. It was like no gas pain I'd ever had, not even after a huge meal of pasta e fagioli. I was scared to do anything, even move. People were all around me, trying to diagnose me. Homeless people were giving second opinions. Finally, someone suggested, "You should go to an emergency room." But by this time, the pain had started to subside, so I said no. I just wanted to go home and lie down.

Two days later, I finally made it to a doctor and he told me I had *mittelschmerz*. I thought he was joking. I said, "Look, I've never had *mittelschmerz* before. Is it anything like *Middlemarch*?" Obviously, he spent his time on the golf course not in the library, and he didn't get the reference. He looked at me as if he had no idea what I was talking about and said, "No." He then proceeded to explain to me that it was this thing that some women have between their periods.

"I'm going to give you painkillers," he said.

So the idiot gave me painkillers and four days later, there I was on the floor again, but this time I was in my apartment, not in a church saying good-bye to Arthur. I was in such horrible pain that my husband called the doctor, who told him to get me in the car right away and take me to the hospital. I didn't want to go to the hospital. I didn't want to go anywhere. I figured, "It's okay. I'll just die here, in familiar surroundings, close to my magazines and videotapes."

My husband wasn't buying this—he probably just wanted me out of the house—so he had to practically carry me to the car. When we got to the hospital I was immediately diagnosed as having an ectopic pregnancy. Apparently homeless people were better diagnosticians than this doctor. I was rushed into the operating room, and the next thing I knew, I was unconscious.

The following day, when I finally woke up, they told me that they'd almost lost me on the operating table and that I was lucky to be alive. In fact, it was that doctor who was lucky to be alive after giving me that ridiculous diagnosis of *mittelschmerz*.

After this near-death experience, I was an entirely different person. I began to identify with the sick and the handicapped. It's a humbling experience, one which I'd recommend to anyone with a character disorder or politicians who continuously veto legislation that would help the less advantaged in this world.

It also changed my outlook on life. In the past, I had been too scared to do anything really risky. I remained in a marriage that had long since passed its expiration date. I had stayed in my job teaching to behavior-challenged high school dropouts, the kind of kids who might have set fire to their parents only to wind up with learning from me the difference between *who* and *whom*. A lot of them had discipline problems in their early lives, but to be fair to them, were now trying to give it a second try and get their high school equivalency diplomas.

Part of the equivalency test was grammar, and I had to teach things like verb and subject agreement Most of these kids couldn't care less if *neither* was a singular subject or a plural subject, but they did want to pass the test. Unfortunately, there were many distractions in their lives. Too many, obviously. One student, Carmen, was a sweet girl with a lot on her mind. Here's a conversation I had with her one day.

Me: Okay, Carmen. Let's go over this. If the subject of the sentence is *everybody,* then the verb in the sentence must be singular because *everybody* is a singular subject.

Carmen: Uh huh.

Me: Let's take the song lyrics, "Everybody's beautiful in their own way." That is incorrect grammar.

Carmen: Joyce, do you think I should remarry my ex-husband?

Me: I don't know, Carmen. Anyway. The correct way to say it would be: Everybody is beautiful in his or her own way. Okay?

Carmen: But, Joyce, (obviously, she couldn't quite grasp the name Joy) we were the envy of the block.

Me: I'm sure you were, Carmen. Now, let's get back to this lesson. Let's say that the subject is *all.* Is that singular or plural?

Carmen: I still love him. We was so happy.

Me: Aha! You don't say, "we was." You say, "we *were* so happy."

Carmen: Joyce, you know, you're a really good teacher.

Me: Thank you, Carmen. Shall we continue?

Carmen: Okay. So, Joyce, should I marry him or what?

As fascinating as this conversation was, it was not how I'd envisioned spending my life. In fact, from the time I was in high school, it was always gnawing at me to be in show business. But I was always too frightened to do it. I'd try, but every time I'd have even the slightest setback, I'd drop it. I remember in college I had to give a speech in class and the topic was "Why Women Should Marry Younger Men." When I first read it aloud in class, I had them rolling in the aisles, so they insisted upon entering me in a speech contest. Suddenly, the circumstances changed. I read my speech, the same speech, only this time nobody was laughing. I bombed. The same thing had happened to me when I was in junior high school and I tried out for the High School of Performing Arts. I passed the first audition with flying colors because there was a large crowd of teachers who laughed at my reading. The second audition was held in front of one woman. She stared at me the whole time and I flubbed my lines and basically stunk up the place. Naturally, I didn't get in. That was pretty much the story of my life. If the audience was with me, I was good. If they weren't, I'd bomb. Simple as that. And I'd take the failure as the truth— that I stunk—and that's the kiss of death when it comes to success. People who are successful take the good and build on it. I'd take the negative and build on that. I was funny in the classroom. I was funny at work. I was funny at parties. My friends would give parties with all sorts of people, and I'd be funny all night—and yet I could not translate that into anything professional, and it was bugging me. I knew I had some kind of talent, but I just couldn't seem to find a way to translate that talent into success. It was driving me bonkers.

The years were rolling by. And then Arthur died. And then I almost died. And then it hit me that dying, really dying, I mean—

in-the-grave-with-a-bunch-of-flowers-on-top-of-it dying, could very possibly be worse than dying onstage in front of a bunch of strangers who would forget your name in an hour.

And that's when I began to transform my life. For one thing, symbolic as it might have been, I decided that the first change, albeit a small one, would be cosmetic: I'd let my hair go natural, from straight to curly. I later found out that straight hair and small noses are what pay off, especially in commercials. One agent at a commercial agency said to me, "Well, you're a good type for Ragu or Driver's Training Institute, but you can't do Procter and Gamble." Then he paused and said, "Well, you can do Procter and Gamble, but you'll have to have the dirty floors. The blondes are the ones who get to have the clean floors." Letting my hair go curly was my way of saying that I was freeing myself from the constraints of convention.

My inspiration for this was the movie *Coming Home* with Jon Voight and Jane Fonda, about our involvement in Vietnam. She had her hair straight in the beginning of the movie and then, suddenly the next day, after spending a night with Jon Voight, her hair curled up. He was a paraplegic, paralyzed from the waist down. Apparently he was not paralyzed from the neck up, and she arose from his bed a new woman, poised to change her life, her marriage, and her hairdo. Jane and I had that in common. The only difference was that she got curly hair from good sex, I got curly hair from a near-death experience. What can we learn from this?

Next, an occupational change. I had show business in mind, so I quit teaching and got a job at "Good Morning America" as a receptionist. Apparently, I was somehow under the impression that the door to show business was to be a receptionist on a television show. As my ex-husband's Aunt Rita used to say, "You'll get your foot in the door." I should have just put my foot in and not my whole body because it was not the most direct route to stardom that I could have come up with.

I did start to force myself to get on stage a little bit more. I went to the Village, appearing in little clubs. As it happened, the gay crowd liked me very much. It was mutual. They were a great audience, laughing at my impression of my Aunt Sadie and my jokes about my hair.

Like Arthur and the rest of the Marxists, they were a great audience, but they were downtown. And although I was making progress, inching my way uptown, virtually block by block, I still had to put food on the table. So, I had to keep my job at "Good Morning America." But I was having fun. Working on a television show is like being in college. You have a lot of laughs. Everybody knows everybody, and everybody is kind of snotty and funny and irreverent and has ADD (attention deficit disorder). They hate television, but at the same time they love it and can't live without it. You love it, and you knock it. That's the way it is.

I may have been having fun, but I wasn't really doing my

job. For one thing, it wasn't particularly challenging. I was way overqualified for this job, which primarily consisted of answering phones for people. It was not my idea of show-biz. I kept wondering why people would call a television show. Didn't they have anything better to do with their time? Didn't they have jobs of their own?

This is what a typical morning manning the phones might be like: The phone would ring. I'd pick it up.

"'Good Morning America.' Hold on, please. Thank you. 'Good Morning America.' Hold on, please. 'Good Morning America.' Hold on, please. David Hartman? He's in the studio. Can I take a message? Oh. Thank you. I'm sure Mr. Hartman would be pleased to hear that.

"'Good Morning America.' Joan Lunden? She wasn't on the air today. She's ill. I think she'll be back tomorrow. I really don't know. Thank you for calling.

"'Good Morning, America.' Oh, hi, sweetie. How are you? What's the matter? Well, ask Daddy where your blue pants are. I think they're in the hall closet. Hold on a second . . . 'Good Morning America.' Miss Lunden has a cold. She'll be back tomorrow.

"Honey, did Daddy find the pants? Tell him to look in the bottom drawer of your room. Don't hang up. I'll be right back.

"'Good Morning America.' Joan Lunden is sick, okay? Get a life.

"'Good Morning America.' Yes. Albert Speer was on this

morning. Yes. Albert Speer, the Nazi. Sir, I don't book the show. Thank you for calling.

"Honey, put Daddy on.

"Joe, her pants are in the bottom drawer. Yes they are. So put another pair on her. It's not up to her. She's eight years old. You're forty-three. I'll call you later.

"'Good Morning America.' Oh, hi, Taffy. You're depressed again? At least you're not suicidal like last week. You are? Hold that thought.

"'Good Morning America.' So, you're calling all the way from Quebec to find out where Joan Lunden is? That's a pretty expensive call. It's worth it? Okay. Hold on. I'll find out." I'd hold the phone for a second. "She has dysmenorrhea. Thank you for calling.

"Taffy, what does your shrink say? She said to call *me*? Look, I can talk, but I can't do your whole life this morning. Hold on . . .

"'Good Morning America.' Yes. We did have an author who claimed that Errol Flynn and Tyrone Power were lovers. Yes, it is shocking. You slept with Tyrone Power? Yeah. Me, too.

"'Good Morning America.' Yes, sir, I agree we shouldn't give airtime to Nazis, but what can I tell you? It's sweeps week.

"Taffy? What about Prozac? Hold on a sec . . .

"'Good Morning America.' Look, Joan Lunden is not here. I don't know where she is. For all I know, she's home sleeping with Albert Speer.

"Taffy, you've got to get out of the house more. I know you're a therapist, but you've got to go somewhere. Hold on.

"Look, he's not the first Nazi to be on TV, and he won't be the last.

" 'Good Morning America.' Yes, Mary Ellen Pinkham did say that you could vacuum the crumbs out of your oven. You got burned? Well, any idiot could figure out that it should be a cold oven. Go ahead and report me. I'll transfer you to my boss. Fine.

" 'Good Morning America.' You want an address for Albert Speer? Try Argentina. And heil Hitler to you, pal.

" 'Good Morning America.' Who gives a crap where Joan Lunden is!

" 'Good Morning America.' Screw you *and* David Hartman.

" 'Good Morning America.' I'm fired? Good. Let Albert Speer answer the phones.

"Taffy, I'll be right over."

So that was my job, but I wasn't *really* fired . . . yet. It took me one year to get promoted to assistant to a producer, a job which was easier and less stressful. Mostly, I was just fooling around a lot and I'd take extended lunch hours to go to psychotherapy twice a week. And by then, I was in psychodrama every Monday night. I was therapizing up the wazoo, because I knew this was my last chance to get myself together, that my life was finite. Up until my near-death experience, I wasn't sure.

But the job was boring and to break the monotony at work, I instituted what they used to call "lesbian hour," which took place at my desk. Every day, at four in the afternoon, all the women in the office would gather around my desk and we'd dish, dish, dish. It got so popular, it was even written about in a book by Ann Northrup, a lesbian activist. Ann wasn't in the closet, but she couldn't believe that straight women were having this lesbian hour, and she later said that it was quite some time before she realized she was the only actual lesbian in attendance. It got so popular, even the men in the office wanted to come, but we wouldn't let them, except for John Bacher, who was brilliant and a man trapped in a woman's problem. And George Merlis, just because we liked him. I always liked George because he hated authority even though he was the executive producer and the ultimate authority at the show. There's something endearing about that.

So now I'm an assistant, I'm going to therapy, I'm sensing that my marriage is on the rocks, I'm not making enough money, I'm unhappy that I'm stuck in my life, and I'm going on commercial auditions. Obviously, with all this going on, I was never at my desk. Who had time to work?

Nevertheless, at one point, I was actually promoted to field researcher, at which time I found out once and for all that I was not cut out for TV production. I had to put together all the elements for a segment of the show, which

Conducting Lesbian Hour.

meant taking care of all the background stuff, like what time everything was going to happen, preinterview the participants, give the producer a thumbnail sketch of what the piece could look like. One of my first assignments was to set up a segment that would show the animals in the Barnum & Bailey Circus walking through the midtown tunnel to get to Madison Square Garden. I did the whole thing, from top to bottom, no problem, smooth as silk. But I made one small mistake: I wrote down 12:00 P.M., instead of 12:00 A.M. I handed it in, all neatly typed, because I did know how to type. I was pretty proud of myself. I was on the fast track to bigger and better things. The next morning, I figured I could go in late because I'd done such a fabulous job. It was about 10:00 A.M. I was in my house putting on makeup, and the phone rang. It was my executive producer.

She said, "Hello, Joy." I said, "Oh, hello," thinking she must be calling to tell me what a fabbo job I did. She said, "Why are you still at home?"

Quick thinker that I am, I said, "Oh, I'm so nauseous. I've been throwing up all morning. I had food poisoning . . ." or whatever other lie I could come up with at the spur of the moment.

"Do you realize, " she said, "that you had the animals marching through the tunnel at *noon* instead of *midnight?*"

"What?" The blood began to rush from my face. I couldn't believe what I was hearing. How could I make such a stupid mistake? Where was my mind? She's going to fire me. I deserve to get fired, I thought. On the other hand, it was just television. It's not like it was life-and-death brain surgery or something. So one part of me is petrified, and the other part of me is saying, It's only television and I almost died three years ago, goddamnit. Fire me.

She didn't fire me that day, so instead, I demoted myself back to answering phones again. I could see that this job was not for me. I was depressed. I still didn't have a way of making a good living. I still wasn't in show business. I still wasn't a comedian. It seemed like a pathetic end. Little did I know that this was really a portentous moment.

One day, not long after I demoted myself, I was called into the executive producer's office. I'd never been called in there before, except when I'd gotten that promotion. But I knew that wasn't going to be the case this time, not after the circus animal screwup. I also knew that I hadn't been at my desk very much and that I'd been generally screwing around. And yet, for some ridiculous reason, I was not prepared for what I was going to hear. Denial is a powerful thing. Look at Mary Jo Buttafuoco standing by her man even with a bullet in her head. Think of all those Mafia wives who believe that their husbands run used-car businesses. I wish doctors would let us have denial back. In the old days, a doctor would never tell you that you were going to die. Never. You could be down to eighty-five pounds and barely breathing, and they'd say, "Oh, yes. Don't forget to come see me in five years for a follow-up."

I went into the executive producer's office and she said, "You know, Joy, we're all very fond of you around here." This was total bullshit. She was not that fond of me. Maybe she was ticked off because she was never invited to lesbian hour. Who knows? So, I said, "You're not going to fire me, are you?" Now, I realize I was just letting her off the hook. Saying something like that only makes it easier for the person doing the evil deed. You wouldn't hand your Manolo Blahniks to a foot fetishist?

I should have let her squirm, because her answer to me was, "Do you think I should?" I said, "No, I don't think you should." "Well, Joy, " she said, "I don't think you're interested in your job . . ." At this point, I burst into tears, which shocked me, because it wasn't as if she was very far off the mark. In fact, if I wasn't so upset, I would have said, "Bingo." But I was a single mother, since the marriage was over at this point, I had no money, and I was scared stiff. What was I going to do? I asked her that question, but she was not a social worker and after all, how could "Good Morning America" continue to stay on the air if I was taking up precious space in the office?

I was in a state of total panic. After I finished crying, I applied for unemployment insurance, which is a blessing from God because unemployment insurance means you don't have to buy lunch, you don't need to have work clothing. I made more money on unemployment than I did when I was working. Not only that, but I got to stay home

My "going away party" at "Good Morning America" (the pink slip is in the cake).

with my daughter, who no longer had to be a latchkey kid.

At the same time this was happening, which was at the end of the summer, a new club was opening in Greenwich Village called Comedy U. The guys who were running it, Burt Levitt and Paul Herzig, had seen me perform and were starting a women's night during the week.

I started appearing there regularly on Thursday nights and then I learned that Lorne Michaels, the producer of "Saturday Night Live," was casting a show called "The New Show." I auditioned for him and got hired. I did a film piece about leaving Brooklyn at the same time. I won a comedy award. And then, six months after being axed from "Good Morning America," I was a guest on the very same show. I couldn't believe it!

My shrink used to say that when you're ready to do something, all the obstacles miraculously disappear, and that's what happened for me. I focused. I got ready. I decided that I had no money, therefore I could not afford to have my ego interfere with anything. If I was bombing onstage, I had to ignore it. I had to get up and do it again, because I needed the money. I believe in the necessity of money. Which, let's face it, is why I could never be a Marxist, even if they did laugh at my jokes.

Random Thought

The Promise Keepers

Only by proclaiming that they are against homosexuality can a group of men openly hug and kiss and cry over one another.

Don't Ask Joy . . . Unless You Want the Real Answer

Q: Dear Joy,

Even though my husband and I have only been married a few months, I find that we're not having sex as often as I thought we would. Do you have any advice?

Judith Claus
St. Louis, Missouri

A: I see your married name is Claus—and yet you're surprised you don't have sex too often. Wake up. Even I know that Santa only comes once a year.

Q: Dear Joy,

My husband is always criticizing me about the size of our phone bill. He says that whenever he turns around, there I am, talking to one of my girlfriends on the telephone. How can I convince him that it's a necessary part of my life and that I'm not going to stop talking on the phone no matter what he says?

Rebecca Adams
San Diego, California

A: That's easy. One night have *all* your girlfriends over to the house—and I mean *all*—and have them talk loud, at the same time, all the time. Believe me, he'll be more than happy to have you on the phone with them instead.

Q: Dear Joy,

I recently graduated college and haven't been able to find a job yet, so I'm still living at home. It's a real nightmare. My parents are really getting on my nerves. Do you have any advice as to how I could get along better with my father and mother?

Sally Goll
Monroe, Wisconsin

A: Of course, Sally. There are three things you should immediately contemplate: 1) Relocation, 2) Relocation, 3) Relocation.

Q: Dear Joy,

I was watching you on TV the other morning and you were on with RuPaul, who was very, very nasty to you. I was wondering what you thought of RuPaul?

Jennifer Johnson
Santa Barbara, California

A: Loved him. Hated her.

Q: Dear Joy, my husband and I have been married for five years and we have a two-year-old child. My husband works long hours, and I just took a job, and so our time together is limited. As a result, our lovemaking has suffered. I know something has to be done, but who do you think should be the one responsible for initiating our love life?

Sarah G.
Sanford, North Carolina

A: The baby-sitter.

Q: Joy,

I've got a *big* problem. I have a boyfriend and we're in love. He thinks I'm smart and beautiful and funny. But I'm afraid that it's all based on a lie, because he doesn't know that I was born a man. I plan on telling him the truth soon, but I need you, Joy. I know you can do it. You're smart and warm and funny and insightful and bitchy (in a good way, of course). *Please!!!*

Samantha Mann
Cleveland, Ohio

A: I have a question for you. Just how small is your penis that your boyfriend has never even noticed? (Bitchy enough for you?)

Women Over Fifty Have It All Together, But Everything Is Falling Apart

I come from a big Italian family where all the women had at least one thing in common: they were all in denial about aging, which is tough to maintain, unless you banish all mirrors from the house.

As soon as Italian women hit forty, the hair miraculously goes blonde, and even more impressive, it somehow manages to stay that way until the coffin is lowered into the ground. In my family, the women die clutching their teeth in one hand and a bottle of Miss Clairol in the other. If pressed, I would have to say that the role model for my female relatives was Zsa Zsa Gabor. You remember her, don't you? Think of "The Merv Griffin Show," because I defy you to come up with any other claim to fame for Ms. Gabor, unless you count allegedly slapping a cop. But as far as my family is concerned, she is a woman to be admired and emulated. First of all, the woman never admits her age. Second of all, she's blonde. And third of all, she is a woman who, though unencumbered by talent, has managed to stay in the spotlight for over fifty years, and yet somehow she has also convinced most of us that she is in her sixties. That's not talent. That's genius! Never mind that her nipples are facing Venezuela. In her eyes, she's a hot babe. And that is good enough for the women in my family.

The women in my old neighborhood did not need to get plastic surgery. Why should they? They had my Aunt Sadie to give them all her beauty tips. "Many people are shocked when I tell them the secrets of my youthful-looking skin," she once told me. "I stay out of the sun or I wear a mantilla on my head at the beach." (Was this when she was dating a bullfighter—in Brooklyn?) "Before I go to bed, " she continued, "I apply a dash of Vagisil to my T-zone." When I asked her about plastic surgery and whether she would ever consider it, she said, "I feel sorry for those women who are not happy with the face that God gave them." She then proceeded to tell me the story of Tessie Abbruzzese, someone she allegedly knew. "Tessie's husband, Frank, said to her one day, 'You got fat, but you got ugly, too. Can't you do something about it?' As if he's such a bargain, with that big wart on his chin." My aunt was strict.

"Anyway," she went on, "Tessie went and got her nose fixed. She had cheeks put in. She had her eyes done and fat sucked out of her arms and thighs. The problem was that after all that surgery, her own dog didn't even recognize her and every time she walked into the house, this overprotective mutt attacked her. One night, she attempted to shoot the dog, and what happened? She killed her husband Frank, instead." Needless to say, this story aroused more than my skepticism. "What happened to Tessie?" I asked.

"Tessie is serving time in a women's prison upstate. She looks fabulous, but for what? Was it worth going through all that pain and expense only to look good for a bunch of women who look exactly like she did before her surgery?" Certainly my aunt has a point here. "And anyway, the only thing wrong with her face was her nose. It was huge. I kept telling her to just wear bigger earrings, but she wouldn't listen to me."

Actually, aging comes upon you gradually, as does menopause and scurvy.

Everyone talks about female menopause, but did you know that we now have books written about male menopause? Apparently, this is a medical phenomenon, not just some psychological made-up notion to sell books. That's right. There's actually a physiological reason why a fifty-year-old man starts wearing banana-colored pants and gold chains around his neck, with his hair parted under his armpit. And don't forget that full-frontal sweep that stands straight up in a strong wind. And yes, there is actually a bona fide medical reason for why that older man across the hall suddenly gets the uncontrollable urge to date twenty-four-year-old women named after lamps, like Tiffany.

I say unto these men that when you feel as if a band of Mexicans has opened up a taco stand on your chest, then we'll talk about menopause.

A lot of men leave their wives during this "menopause." And with the invention of the new drug Viagra, the exodus is becoming epidemic. What with this newfound sense of machismo, a lot of these geezers are finding that life is worth living again, but not with the wife that stuck around when the Goodyear blimp was limp. This new drug is not all it's cracked up to be. I happen to have come upon a diary that was kept by one woman during the Viagra madness days. I thought I would share it with you here.

Diary of a Mad Viagra Housewife

Day 1

Just celebrated our twenty-fifth wedding anniversary although there wasn't much to celebrate. When it came time to reenact our wedding night, *he* was the one who locked himself in the bathroom and cried.

Day 2

Today he says he has a big secret to tell me. I couldn't imagine what it was, but I knew it wasn't good because he took a double dose of Prozac tonight. Then he breaks the news. He's impotent, he says, and he wants me to be the first to know. Why doesn't he tell me something I *don't* know. I mean, gimme a break. He's been dysfunctional for so long, he even *walks* with a limp.

Day 3

This marriage is in trouble. A woman has needs. Yesterday, I saw a picture of the Washington Monument and burst into tears.

Day 4

A miracle has occurred. There's a new drug on the market that will fix his "problem." It's called Viagra. I told him that if he takes Viagra, things will be just like they were on our wedding night. He said, "This time I'd rather not have your mother join us." (I think this will work. I replaced his Prozac with the Viagra hoping to lift something other than his mood.)

Day 5

He took it and boy did it work! He's so impressed with himself, he's taken to calling it Trump Tower.

Day 6

This Viagra thing has gone to his head. (No pun intended.) Yesterday at Burger King, the manager asked me if I'd like a Whopper. He thought they were talking about him. *Get over yourself!* Not everything is about you.

Day 7

I think he took too many over the weekend. Yesterday, instead of mowing the lawn, he was using his new friend as a weed whacker.

Day 8

I don't have much time to write. I hear him calling me again. You know how people say they wouldn't touch you with a ten-foot pole? I wish that's what *he* thought.

Day 9

Okay, I admit it. I'm hiding. I mean, a girl can only take so much. The photo of Janet Reno isn't working. What am I gonna do?

Day 10

The side effects are starting to get to him. He says that everything is turning blue. The other day we were watching Kenneth Branagh in *Hamlet* and he thought it was *The Smurfs Do Denmark*.

Day 11

I'm basically being drilled to death. It's like being married to Black and Decker.

Day 12

I wish he was gay. I bought 400 Liza Minnelli albums and I keep saying "fabulous," and still he keeps coming after me.

Day 13

Now I know how Saddam Hussein's wife feels. Every time I shut my eyes, there's a sneak attack. It's like going to bed with a Scud missile. Let's hope he's like President Bush and he pulls out in a hundred days.

Day 14

I've done everything to turn him off. Nothing is working. I even started dressing like a nun. Now he tells me Sister Wendy revs his motor.

Day 15

I may just have to kill him. Then he'll go out the way he wants to: stiff.

My Aunt Sadie gave a great deal of advice to me about men. Too bad I didn't listen. She'd say, "A man who is denied regular access to his wife's pasture will often seek out other fields to plow." (And the woman never set foot on a farm!) "I realize," she'd say, "that there are many, many, many nights you are just not in the mood for s-e-x. One method that has worked is to train yourself to concentrate on something that *does* interest you. For instance, on a night when your husband is in a state of individual arousal, try to mentally clean the refrigerator. That way you can satisfy your husband while preventing moldy buildup on the provolone."

It's interesting to observe what often happens when a man walks out on a thirty-five-year marriage. At first, the wife is devastated. "How will I go on? I don't have a job. I'm nothing. Everybody has a husband." But wait. You see these same women three or four years later and they're going for their Ph.D.s They're sporting Armani jackets and they're attending the Visconti retrospective at Lincoln Center's Walter Reade Theatre. They're writing a book on the joys of divorce and they're having orgasms again (with or without a man).The husband, who left because he fell for a twenty-year-old who was impressed with his knowledge of Chinese cuisine (especially the Dumpling King) is now walking around wearing loafers without socks, on his way to see *Dumb and Dumber*. His girlfriend is whining, "Like, I don't wanna go to another museum. I don't wanna see another exhibit. I hate Lucien Freud. Let's go to a Snoop Doggy Dogg concert."

Having said all that, I still like my men a little younger than me. Since women live an average of seven years longer than men, I figure, why spend my last days without someone to massage my feet while I'm on the phone. And I'm not ready for the conversations with old guys.

"Don't forget to comb your lobes, Murray," is not my idea of scintillating chatter. I went out with this older man, very nice, but he had to get up to pee forty times a night. It makes you paranoid. At first you think he has a kidney problem. Then you start to think, The guy is cheating on me . . . in the bathroom.

Many things are much easier for older guys than they are for the older women. Like propagation of the species. Take Tony Randall. The man is in his late seventies, and married to a young woman of twenty-seven! They had a second child. I have to give him credit. This was all done pre-Viagra. Also, Charlie Chaplin, Anthony Quinn, and Pablo Picasso are three other famous men who became fathers as the last drop of spermatozoa dribbled out. Talk about your trickle down theory! Everyone applauds their performances and thinks little of the fact that their wives may have to change diapers for fathers and children at the same time.

But think of the kids. On Open School Night, they'll be the only ones whose fathers are asking the teachers why the desks don't have inkwells.

On the other hand, there are a few women, some in their fifties and some in their sixties, who are also becoming mothers at this late date. These women are usually carrying eggs of young women, but they do get pregnant and they do deliver babies.

One woman carried her daughter's eggs and gave birth to her own grandchild. Now, I know that grandmothers like to baby-sit, but in their uterus? At any rate, the world is fairly horrified by these postmenopausal women popping out these kids.

Personally I don't care what they do, but I can tell you right now that when I'm seventy-five, I don't want to be watching reruns of *Baywatch* with a horny teenage boy that I gave birth to.

There are, however, certain things I like about getting older. For one thing, if you're getting married, the phrase "'til death do you part," doesn't sound so horrible. It only means about ten or fifteen years and not the freaking eternity it used to mean. I've even begun to like the hot flashes. It's like being in love again without the aggravation. When I was twenty, *plastic* was a dirty word. Now it's something I can really believe in—especially when it has the word *surgeon* after it. I now have the maturity to deal with the fact that my body is falling apart.

We women also are more into reality concerning men. When we were in our twenties and thirties we were looking for a guy who was perfect. He had to be handsome, tall, funny, smart, a wonderful lover who would make a great father, and of course, with excellent earning potential. He could cook a paella and dance the fandango. He would have stock tips and be able to balance the checkbook while changing a fuse. We now know that this man does not exist. All we want now is a guy who's good in bed and not annoying when he's not in bed.

Don't Ask Joy . . . Unless You Want the Real Answer

Q: Dear Joy,

I'm Catholic and the man I'm going to marry is Jewish. I know that you, too, are Catholic and that you were once married to a Jewish guy. Do you have any advice for me on how to make a mixed marriage work?

Susie Lopez
Miami Beach, Florida

A: Susie—you are in for a fabulous marriage! A Catholic girl and a Jewish guy—do you have any idea how easy it's going to be to make him feel guilty? You'll have him in the palm of your hand in no time. Also, I see you're from Florida, that's

67

so convenient—in fifty years you won't have to retire to Florida. You'll already be there.

Q: Dear Joy,

I've got a terrible secret that I've been keeping from my husband, and it's eating me up alive. I'm a lesbian. When do you think is the best time to tell him?

Patti
New York City

A: The best time would have been the moment just before you said, "I do." Failing that, try to time it around when your car needs a major tune-up and overhaul. This way, either he'll be so preoccupied with the car that he won't care if you're a lesbian, *or* he'll figure, being a lesbian *you* can fix the car, and save him a coupla hundred bucks.

❀   ❀   ❀

Q: Dear Joy,

I've got a good job, a loving husband, and both my kids are now out of the house. Finally, after all these years of anxiety, everything seems to be the way I'd always imagined it could be and I'm actually content with my life. What's wrong with me?

Robin Burns
Syracuse, New York

A: I don't know—but do you see a bright, white light at the end of a tunnel?

Q: Dear Joy,

I just graduated from college a few months ago and although I did pretty well and my mother is proud of me—I made the dean's list—she keeps nagging me about getting a "real job." Every time I turn around, there she is, criticizing me: I'm lazy. I drink too much. My hair's too long. My friends are losers. The girls I go out with aren't any good. How do I get her off my back and tell her to mind her own damn business—in a nice way?

Stephen W.
Houston, Texas

A: Two words: Lyle Menendez.

Random Thought

Pornography

Men love to watch two women make love. I wonder, does this turn them on or are they just trying to figure out how to do it right?

Eight Minutes
of Terror

I once read a report in the newspaper that investigators found that when a Korean airline jet went down in 1983, the passengers knew they were going to die for eight minutes. That's eight minutes of terror. Eight minutes of heart-stopping, alert, conscious, life-flashing-before-your-eyes terror.

In the name of science (and personal curiosity), I took it upon myself to find out what eight minutes really feels like. First, I applied some Nair to my upper lip to get rid of some mustache hairs and timed it. By six minutes, my lip was starting to burn. But an experiment is an experiment, and so rather than wipe it off, I stubbornly allowed it to stay there. The next two minutes were an eternity. But somehow I made it through.

Okay. No problem. Obviously, I could, if I put my mind

to it, handle eight minutes of terror; or at least my upper lip could. And so, with this in mind, I said yes to a job that would entail covering thirteen American cities in three weeks' time. That meant that I would have to take fifteen airplane flights.

Believe me, I know all the clichés, among them that it's safer in a plane than it is in a car. After all, the reasoning goes, there are zillions of flights every day, and how many actually crash? And when people hear that you don't like to fly, they suddenly become amateur therapists. "Well, if you don't like to fly, Joy, I guess you've got serious control problems, don't you?" Blah blah blah.

And believe me, I use all these same arguments when I'm ready to take to the air. But the truth is, when you're actually ready to take off and you hear a strange noise, none of these rationalizations work.

"What was that noise?" I hear myself exclaim aloud as we are about to leave Detroit on a 727. Nobody answers me. I say it again. "What was that noise?" The other passengers are mute, either oblivious to the strange noise, or a bunch of acquiescent sheep that make cloning irrelevant.

Suddenly, the captain's voice fills the cabin, explaining, "You'll be hearing a loud noise upon takeoff because *wfeferslueklued*."

"What was that?" I ask, of no one in particular. And no one, either in particular or in general, answers. I am in a panic. Everyone is strapped in. The stewardess (by this time,

I couldn't care less if they now like to call themselves flight attendants) is still standing at the front of the cabin. Like a flash, seatbelt sign or not, I bolt out of my seat. I walk forward, toward the flight deck, and ask of the stewardess, who by this time is explaining flotation devices, "What did he say?" Obviously irritated that I've dared leave my seat in the middle of her flight demonstration, not to mention disobeying seatbelt-fastened regulations, she repeats the idiot pilot's remark. "But what does that mean?" I ask.

"Ma'am, the pilot wouldn't take off if it weren't safe." Ha! Am I to believe that? After all, isn't there a damn good chance that the pilot of that ill-fated Korean plane thought it was safe to take off?

She tells me to sit down and so, fearing risk of being arrested by the FBI, I obey her. But my mind is racing at high speed. *I could get off,* I tell myself. *I could just say to the stewardess, the pilot, the copilot, the navigator, whoever the hell tries to stop me, Look, I want to get off.* That's it. I could do that, you know. I could just stand up and say, *Let me off this plane. I have made a decision to get off. You all can stay on if you want to. I am choosing to get off.* They would have to let me off. This is not a dictatorship. I have free will. For God's sake, this is America!

But somehow my butt is still nailed to that damn seat. Still, that doesn't stop me from thinking about all the people on all the other planes throughout the history of aviation that have gone down. Amelia Earhart. Patsy Cline. Ricky

Nelson. Buddy Holly. John Denver. Those soccer players who went down in the Andes and wound up eating each other. If they were alive, surely each would be thinking now, *If only I had gotten off at the last minute. If only I had said, Let me off this plane. If I had done that, I wouldn't now be noshing on this kneecap. I just heard a funny noise and I have a feeling it's going to crash.*

I once met a guy who told me that a friend of his had missed a flight because his wife was late, and that the plane he was supposed to be on crashed. He has the ticket framed in his living room. Sitting there in my seat waiting to take off, my knuckles turning white as I crush the armrest between my fingers, I suddenly recall something that happened to me before I got on the plane. I was standing in the boarding area and the attendant looked at my ticket. "Did you check in?" she asked.

"Yes, why?" I answer, nervously.

"Well, there's no stamp on it."

Now I wonder, was that a sign? Was that the fateful moment that I will look back on as we descend, nose first, into the Rockies?

This is my moment. I could say, "Let me off! Now." I could save my life. My daughter would not be a half an orphan. My friends would not have to attend my wake and say things like, "Poor Joy, gone in the prime of life. Just when people were beginning to understand her humor."

"You know, she was no kid. She was already getting hot flashes."

"After all the years of struggle, she's finally beginning to make it and her plane crashes."

My mind wanders to the day before I embarked on this thirteen-city job. I called my Aunt Rose. She was ninety-one. She came over from Turin when she was ten years old and remained in Brooklyn, in the same neighborhood, for eighty-one years. She worked in a factory as a merrow operator on sweaters. I thought I would give her a ring because she was homebound and she liked to hear from me.

When she answered the phone, I asked, "How are you feeling?" which is the same question I asked every time I spoke to her. "Like that," she replied, which is the same answer I always got.

"How's the arthritis?"

"I can hardly walk anymore."

The woman has never flown in a plane; she has never sailed on a boat (except for the trip from Turin) and she doesn't like trains. "I saw a train in a movie that went off a bridge and everybody drowned," she once told me, explaining her aversion to railroads. The odd thing is, she has absolutely no fear of cars. She would not fly, she would not take a train, yet she would drive with her legally blind husband.

When I told her about my thirteen-city tour, and the fact that I would have to do a lot of flying, she said, "Oh, my God. Don't do it. Don't you read about all those planes crashing?"

I deftly slipped on my cliché hat. "Oh, Aunt Rose. Do you

know how many planes take off every day? From all over the world? Thousands. Millions. How many actually crash? One every year, maybe."

"What about that TWA flight that blew up over Long Island last year?" she countered, cutting through my silly statistics like a seamstress with a machete.

"Well, of course, anything can happen. You could get hit by a car walking to the bread store. You could get hit in the head by a falling air conditioner."

"Yes," she answered, with irrefutable logic, "but you would be on the ground when it happened."

My mother was a fatalist. She believed that whatever was to be, was to be. Like St. Augustine, predestination was her overriding philosophy. "When it's your time to die, you'll die," she used to say. *"Che sarà, sarà."* She was the Doris Day of Brooklyn. Naturally, I used to question this.

"But Ma, what if I'm on a plane, and it's the pilot's time to die?"

Her answer was startling and never failed to stop me in my tracks. "Do you want steak or chicken for dinner?"

My mother was born in Pennsylvania, but when her mother died in childbirth, her father took her back to Calabria. It was there that she remained for thirteen long years and it was there that she learned the art of coping. Talismans: garlic around the neck for evil spirits. Phrases to live by: "Don't spit up in the air. It comes back in your face." Advice: "Never admit (to yourself or anyone else) that something good is happening, because then something bad will happen."

By this time my mind is back in the present. I have not bullied my way off the plane, and by this time we are somewhere high over Indiana and the stewardess is bent over my seat, trying to calm me. She is smiling that Friendly Skies smile. "The noise the pilot was talking about was related to the air-conditioning system," she explains sweetly.

"You mean it had nothing to do with the engine that flies this thing?" I ask.

"That's right, " she says, as she straightens up and begins to walk away.

"She could have told me that before we took off, " I say, aloud to the sheep clone next to me, who doesn't even bother to look up from his copy of *Money* magazine.

I hate everyone.

Joy's Travelogue

Picnics in the Cemetery

After ten years of therapy, I finally am able to take trips without medication. My reluctance to travel came because I was and am a product of my upbringing, and I happen to know that Italians do not like to travel. These are not the Vikings we're discussing here, but the Italians who will make the arduous trip from Calabria, go to Avenue Z in Brooklyn, and then remain there for the next fifty years.

This is not to say that this penchant for nesting is a bad thing. When other ethnic groups are fleeing to the suburbs, the Italians stay put and take care of their neighborhoods, albeit with a vengeance.

The negative side of this was that as a child I never really got to go on vacation. While other American kids were going to camp in the summer, I was hanging out at a mozzarella store, or playing jacks on the roof, or just sweating. For us, the roof was like a giant resort. Movies were shown up there at night, and during the day people would sunbathe, as if it were the French Riviera. Occasionally, some pervert would expose himself to us and we would go screaming down the stairs. (Ah, yes. Sweet memories!)

Sometimes my family would go so far as to try to pass the cemetery off as a trip to the country. A hot day would arrive and my Aunt Sadie would say, "Come on, Joy. Let's go visit Grandma and Grandpa." I was not a stupid kid. I knew Grandpa and Grandma were dead. I went to the wake, didn't I? But I figured, what the hell, it'll get me off the stoop and I'd get to ride in my Uncle Dickie's pink Caddy to St. John's Cemetery in Queens, which I thought was a suburb. My Aunt Sadie was always the cheerful optimist and when I'd grouse about it, she'd say, "You've got grass, you've got trees. Who's better than you?"

I learned gardening in the cemetery and I also posed for many snapshots. A lot of photos were taken at St. John's, in an attempt, perhaps, to capture the moment in case *Mausoleum Monthly* called.

Please, God, let them take
me on a real vacation.

Finally, a real vacation.

Watch (What You Say) on the Rhine

A few years ago, a popular radio show that broadcasts from Boston asked me if I would like to go to Munich for Oktoberfest. We would do the show from Germany, but only Boston would hear it. This seemed like an expensive way to do a radio show. Why not just have some boot sounds in the background and stay in Boston? Who would know that we weren't in Germany?

The powers that be thought I was crazy when I made this suggestion, but they still wanted me to go. It was a radio show. Everybody on radio is crazy!

Oktoberfest is held in September (and I'm the crazy one?). It's one big party during which time thousands of Germans gather in these huge halls and sing German songs, drink German beer, and pee German pee. The whole crowd sways back and forth in unison as they sing such Bavarian favorites as "Deutschland, Deutschland Über Alles." The robust beer maids carry up to five steins of beer in each hand. No small feat, since you could drown a dachshund in one of these mugs.

We all squeezed into the mayor of Munich's reserved table overlooking a sea of tow-headed crew cuts. They gave us the VIP treatment, thinking that this was a big deal show and not the morning-drive wacko hour that it really was. Everyone at the table immediately ordered a small beer (which for Germans meant less than a quart), but I've never really acquired a taste for the suds, so I asked the waitress for a glass of chardonnay. When she stopped laughing, she said something like "Wein es verboten in Oktoberfest." It was then that I realized that I was in the wrong room, so I dragged my boyfriend out of there and went to a nearby restaurant, making sure not to trip over any Oktobersots.

I was finally able to get a glass of wine and a lovely poached salmon in a very refined restaurant. It was like going from a Rolling Stones concert to a string quartet recital at the Cloisters. Two drinks later my mind started to wander. Suddenly, I heard myself saying to no one in particular, "Gee, do you think there are any Nazis here?" Well, apparently my voice carries because suddenly you could hear a *stecknadel* (pin) drop. Everyone in the restaurant suddenly stopped talking and turned to stare at me. The vibe in the room had definitely turned unfriendly. It was then that I deduced that I might have committed a faux pas.

Oktoberfest in *September*—hello?

As the paranoia mounted and my boyfriend's Jewish survival instinct kicked in, we quickly asked for the check and got out, all the while making sure that no one was following us. They weren't, but we certainly learned a lesson which I will pass on to you now. Germans do not like the word *Nazi*. They're sick of it, they feel guilty, they're in deep denial. Whatever.

What? Did I make this word up? Am I the one who created this concept? Am I to be blamed because the whole country needs therapy? I don't think so. But a word to the wise is sufficient. If you ever find yourself in Germany, don't use the word *Nazi*. Don't even say, "Wanna play a game of Yahtzee." They don't want to hear it. Especially the older ones with the eye patches and the limps.

You get the picture.

Going Down
on a Mule

The Grand Canyon is one of those natural wonders that puts you in your place. Its majestic immensity reminds you that you are very tiny indeed and that compared to that big hole in the ground, you are but an insignificant speck of dust.

But after you get over this feeling, you realize it's just another theme park with mule rides. They have these indentured mules who apparently are very sure-footed because they go down these precipitous, narrow paths all the way to the bottom of the canyon, with idiot tourists riding on their backs. Why do these people have to go down the canyon on these animals? What do they expect to see down there and why can't they look at it from a safe distance?

There's no way I would ever mount a mule, particularly if there was no place to shop at the end of the ride. When I visited the Grand Canyon I kept thinking, What if this mule puts it into its head to jump? You're on a suicidal mule and you don't even know it. These poor beasts cannot take another sack of overweight flesh on their backs.

I'm almost positive I heard one of them saying, "If one more fat tub gets on top of me, I'm jumping."

Besides, I don't trust an animal that wears a hat with holes in it for its ears.

You Can't Count on Monte Cristo

I studied French in college so that I would not sound stupid when I ordered snails. Some phrases are easy to master such as *Où est la bibliothèque?* (Where is the library?) Or *Voulez vous couchez avec moi?* (Will you go to bed with me?)

But trying to count in French is a whole other magillah. This is the way you say the number ninety-nine in French: Quatre-vingt-dix-neuf. Or, four times twenty plus nineteen. You actually have to add and multiply these numbers.

Now, it should be said, in all fairness, that I was not a good math student, even in English. I wouldn't know the difference between a cosine and a stop sign, so you can imagine how difficult it was for me when I had to translate all of these mental calculations.

Let us not excuse the French here. They are annoying and we all know it. When I was in Paris, I had to go to the hotel

Me and a fan on the rue de Jerry Lewis.

which, believe it or not, was at 99 rue de Jerry Lewis. Since I could not remember "quatre-vingt-dix-neuf," I innocently said to the driver, "Neuf neuf." The guy thought there was a hare-lipped dog in the backseat. "Neuf neuf" I kept yelling, until he finally got it.

"*Ah, oui,*" he yelled back, "*vous est très jolie.*" The French may be annoying, and they may hate deodorants, but they are not stupid!

After being pulled over by the LAPD.

California
Screaming

When you travel to California, be aware that they have certain rules of the road that may be different from what you are accustomed to. On my first trip to Los Angeles, I was not told that it is the law to stop for pedestrians whenever and wherever they are crossing the street. You would think they would post this information at the airport, wouldn't you.

I picked up my rent-a-car at LAX and cruised up La Cienega. Some guy started to cross the street and I went right past him. He yelled out "bitch." I turned around and I said to myself, I wonder if there's somebody here who knows me.

Random Thought

Hollywood

I was watching the Academy Awards and
I noticed that when the camera panned the
audience you could plainly see that the plastic
surgeon's scalpel must have been working
overtime. Maybe we should just call it The
Night of a Hundred Scars.

Chestnuts Roasting on an Open Friar

In 1997, I was chosen to be the first woman to host a Friars Club roast. Some people might think this is no big deal, but they're wrong. Getting men to listen to a woman is hard enough, but getting them to laugh when a woman is telling the joke is right up there with getting them to dust the furniture.

For those of you who are not familiar with the Friars Club, let me give you some background. The Friars Club is a "fraternal" organization with a large roster of showbiz luminaries, including Frank Sinatra and Irving Berlin, to name but two of the most famous, though deceased, members.

From 1902 until 1988, the Friars Club was open only to men. For some reason, women were anathema to these guys. What were they so afraid of? Did they think we would stop them from scratching their behinds in the dining room, or possibly give away the secret formula of the Friars red dye used on many members' heads?

In 1996 I was thrilled to be asked to join a club whose members included performers whom I had admired and respected all through my childhood and adult life. To belong to the same club as Jack Benny, George Burns, Phyllis Diller, Joan Rivers, and many, many other truly funny and talented performers was thrilling. I could now walk through the Milton Berle Room and watch Professor Irwin Corey pontificate on the evils of capitalism and the heartbreak of constipation. I could now eat lunch with a guy named Dennis Stein (whose main claim to fame was that he once dated Elizabeth Taylor) and the comedian Freddie Roman, the dean of the Friars and frequent MC of club fund-raisers. Freddie often gave us useful elocution lessons. My favorite has always been the night he thanked the audience "on behalf of all the comedians." Apparently, Freddie took the phrase, "Think Yiddish, talk British" to heart.

And of course I could now schmooze with Henny Youngman, who ate lunch at the club every day and always had a one-liner to share.

The Friars Club roasts are part of the club's tradition and probably the single most notorious aspect of the club's history. Every year, the club would select a celebrity and members would do their utmost to verbally abuse and humiliate him and all the others on the dais in the raunchiest way possible. The proceeds usually go to the roastee's favorite charity. It was a men's-only affair until 1983, at the Sid Caesar roast, when Phyllis Diller disguised herself as a guy and crashed. Everyone said she was a dead ringer for Claude Rains. No one realized that it was Phyllis until she went into the men's room whereupon she was spotted by one of the attendees. A year later, Buddy Hackett was hosting an event at the club and he said, "All of you feel around and if you don't feel balls, please stand up." In 1985, Phyllis Diller was admitted back into the club as the guest of honor. The floodgates were opened and women have been invading the place with great enthusiasm ever since. Thank you, Phyllis.

Many of the men still don't love having us there, but we don't care. We're there and they have to deal with it. Often, on our way out of the dining room, we would hear comments such as, "It was better before. It's not the club it once was." Or "There go the yentas." Nevertheless, things have changed. In the beginning, the men would only let us use the gym on Tuesday and Thursday mornings. Personally, this was a nonissue for me, but since we paid the same dues, we didn't think this was fair. But all they had were men-only facilities. Finally, one of the women members suggested we all shower and sauna together. The thought of us seeing them naked was enough to cause them to spend one-and-a-half million dollars to renovate and create separate facilities. Now they're used to us. First they wanted to keep us out. Now they can't stay away from our lunch table because the best dishing goes on there.

Phyllis Diller or Claude Rains?

People remember the Whoopi Goldberg/Ted Danson roast where Ted showed up in blackface and uttered racial epithets. He shocked the media (along with some of the guests including Montel Williams, who walked out in a huff). This negative reaction was considered a major annoyance by the members, since the roasts are private and therefore not supposed to be open to the press. Plus, political correctness has never been the hallmark of Friars roasts. In fact, the opposite is true and comedians have scrupulously guarded this privilege for years. Political correctness is the enemy of humor and the roasters not only guard their tradition of lambasting one another as well as revered institutions, but they also revel in the ribaldry. It's dirty and we love it.

I was asked to host the roast in honor of Danny Aiello. Who can forget his rendition of the strict father in Madonna's video *Papa Don't Preach*? or the pizza shop owner in Spike Lee's movie, *Do the Right Thing*? I knew that I wanted to strike a tone that was in the tradition of the previous roasts: bawdy but with a feminine touch. Not easy, considering that I didn't want members to think that I had chickened out. At the same time, I walk a very thin line as a woman. Many "blue" jokes are more easily accepted by an audience when they are spoken by men than when they come out of the mouth of a woman. I never understood this, because nothing is raunchier than a bunch of women at a bridal shower, so it's the men's problem. Anyway, I got up to the podium, faced the three thousand predominantly male faces, took a deep breath, and began . . .

"Here I am, the first woman to be selected as a roast master in the history of the Friars Club. I, in turn, offer my congratulations. Welcome to the sixteenth century. Actually, it's quite an honor to be the first female roastmaster in ninety-three years. Which is ironic, because ninety-three is the average age of most of the Friars.

"At this point, to me, the Friars Club is just a gay bar without the good-looking guys.

"Before they let women in the club, the place was like Yeshiva University where everybody majored in phlegm.

"A lot of Friars thought that it would be a big risk to ask a woman to host the roast. I think they chose me because even though I'm a woman, they think I have big brass balls. That happens to be true. My balls are brassier than the ones in Joey Adams's hips.

"They all thought that with my reputation of being so 'ladylike and genteel' that I wouldn't be able to get down to the level of raunchiness that all these old cocksuckers are used to. Well, I say screw that. I'll do the best I can, given my elegant track record.

"We are here today to honor and rip to shreds an actor we all know and love: Danny Thomas. Unfortunately he's dead, so we settled for Danny Aiello, a friendly man, a loving father, a devoted husband, a man whose motto has always been: 'I'm Danny Aiello, who the hell are you?'

"Danny began his career in show business as a bouncer at the original Improvisation comedy club. He took that experience and used it to his advantage. While a lot of actors in Hollywood need plastic surgery, Danny Aiello causes it. This guy has knocked out more teeth than Michael Spinks has in his mouth.

"Over the years, Danny and I have had many political arguments. His politics are slightly to the right of Benito Mussolini. In fact, his nickname is 'Il Duce Bag.'

"It's obvious that Danny is in love with himself. His wife tells me he walks around the house naked. He answers the doorbell naked. She said he comes up to her bed every morning and asks, 'Want some coffee, honey?' Yeah, Danny. She wants the coffee, but you can keep the stirrer.

"We've got some other people here tonight, to honor Danny. Here's Robert Klein, whose career has been so diversified that he's performed more different acts than Heidi Fleiss.

"And, of course, it is an honor to have Barbara Walters on the dais tonight. What can I say about Barbara Walters? In addition to being an award-winning journalist, Barbara is a TV icon. She is an ABC News special correspondent, she is coanchor of ABC News' magazine '20/20.' She hosts The Barbara Walters specials; she is a contributor to ABC News' 'Turning Point'; she's the coexecutive producer and panelist on 'The View'; She played Darren on 'Bewitched,' and twice a week she helps Robin Williams wax his back. This is a very busy woman.

"In addition to all this, she has written books and raised a daughter. I understand that next year, Barbara plans to bring peace to the Middle East, repair the hole in the ozone layer, and wash the feet of the poor.

"It's also nice to be in a room with Renee Taylor when she and Joe Bologna are not throwing a wedding for themselves. These two have taken more vows than the Carmelite nuns. Renee, I have to tell you: Stop the pathetic plea for gifts. If you need a blender, I'll just call the Wiz and have them send one over.

"A lot of people say Pat Cooper is too angry. I say, hey, what's the problem? He compensates for being angry by being bitter. The man has done more backbiting than Marv Albert. Throughout his long and lucrative career, Pat has had the opportunity to share the stage with such superstars as Tony Bennett, Frank Sinatra, Paul Anka, and Jerry Lewis, and he has resented the money they made off of him ever since.

"The truly amazing thing about Jerry Orbach is that, in spite of starring in 'Law and Order,' *Broadway Bound, Dirty Dancing, Prince of the City, Crimes and Misdemeanors, Chicago,* and *42nd Street,* still, nobody has any idea who he is."

Everyone took my ribbing in good spirits until I had to introduce Sandra Bernhard. All I said was, "What is it exactly that you do?" At which point, she rushed up to the podium and practically pushed me off the dais and into Buddy Hackett's soup. Apparently, she wanted to kill me. Oh, well, I guess I won't be invited to any of her major off-off-Broadway openings. (It's a joke, Sandra, okay?)

I went on a bit longer and introduced the next roaster and the evening was a huge hit. Richard Belzer was merciless toward Danny Aiello. Instead of preparing material, Richard read verbatim from some of the reviews of Danny's now defunct show, "DellaVentura, " which were, to say the least, scathing. Apparently Danny had not read these reviews and he was devastated to learn how much the critics detested the show and his performance. When he got up to speak at the end of the roast, as is traditional, instead of giving as good as he got, he broke down and cried like Jimmy Swaggart on a bad night. Danny is an emotional guy, but no one likes to see a big bruiser cry, and we proceeded to demolish him at the party at the club after the roast was over. All in all, it was a ball.

After it was over, I not only felt relieved, but it was as if I had actually grown a penis. Thank God it was a hallucination because I have a hard enough time getting in my pants as it is.

Random Thought

Eating Disorders

Anorexia is just another word for nothing left to lose.

Don't Ask Joy . . .
Unless You Want
the Real Answer

Q: Dear Joy,

There's this guy who is a friend of one of my girlfriends. The thing is, I'm really attracted to him, but whenever all of us are together as a group he doesn't seem to notice me. Do you have any advice as to how I can get him to pay attention to me?

Joyce O'Dwyer
Omaha, Nebraska

A: Surprise him. Invite him over to your place and when he comes to your door make sure you're wearing a really sexy outfit—a micromini with stiletto heels and fishnets comes to mind. If he says, "Wow! That dress is great—you look so hot," you've done it! If he says, "Wow! That dress is great—does it come in *my* size?"—introduce him to your brother.

Q: Dear Joy,

Sometimes my husband acts like an idiot. And from my experience, he's not alone. Tell me, Joy, how can men be so stupid?

Caroline R.
Orlando, Florida

A: That's simple, Caroline. Frequently—all *too* frequently—the blood drains from a man's head and travels south, leaving him with nothing upstairs.

Q: Dear Joy,

My husband and I have been married for five years, but his first wife is driving us crazy. She just refuses to leave us alone. She's constantly interfering in our lives. She's even gone so far as to threaten us. I'm really afraid that it's just a matter of time before she's going to do something really dangerous. What can we do?

Wendy
Portland, Maine

A: Tell her she has to sleep on the couch until she learns to control herself. If that doesn't work, I'm afraid you'll just have to ask her to move out.

Cherie I with my
mother.

Cherie III

Cherie II

Dogs I Have Known

A Photo Essay

Cheries I, II, and III

Aunt Rose was partial to poodles and, whether male or female, she called them "Cherie."

Pudgy

Pudgy was the one and only dog I ever had as a child. Unfortunately, he lasted only a week because my mother couldn't tolerate his eating the furniture.

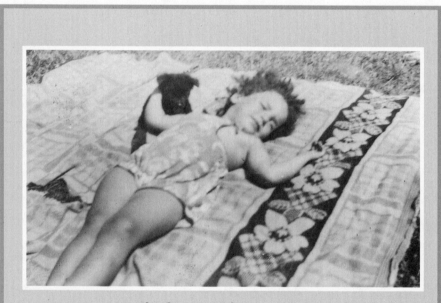

More suntan oil, please, and a credenza for Pudgy.

Phoebe and Molly

Two female basset hounds that were trapped at Exit 60 with me.

They beat the boredom by falling in love with each other.

A reʌult of the love that dare not ʌpeak itʌ name.

Max

Max is the dog my daughter and I adopted. He's been spayed, and yet he insists on humping anyone who comes close enough.

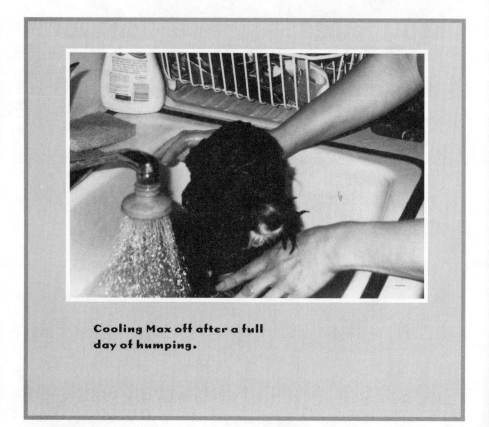

Cooling Max off after a full day of humping.

Random Thought

Learning Disabilities

Is it easier to read Hebrew if you're dyslexic?

Marriage and Other Gambles

My boyfriend and I have been going together for more than fifteen years and every so often the subject turns to marriage, or, at least moving in together. It would certainly be the financially smart thing to do and his constant travelling back and forth between apartments would be cut down, not to mention the relentless search for parking spots and the packing and unpacking.

After ten years of being together, and his constantly carrying a bag to my house, one day he realized that I had an entire drawer in my dresser devoted only to shoulder pads. It was at this point that he uttered those six words that never fail to send shivers up my spine: "I think we need to talk." He then proceeded to explain his position: "I don't wanna be pushy, but after all this time, why am I schlepping this bag when I know that those are disposable shoulder pads and they have a drawer of their own? I'm not talking about moving in, but don't you think you can move those pads in with your underwear?"

At first, I was reluctant. After all, I figured that if I gave up a drawer, could a closet be far behind? And would this be the first step down that slippery path toward never being able to say those words that I cherish so dearly: "Honey, I think it's time for you to go home now."

But it seemed incredibly selfish of me to keep those pads there in the face of such a rational request, so I relented.

Time has proven my fears to be founded. He not only has his own drawer, he has his own night table, and a section of my closet, not to mention a shelf in the medicine chest. His laundry gets done once a week, I have a dog that he makes out with constantly without any of the expenses (food, grooming, medical) associated with owning a dog, and when he's too lazy to get a haircut, I shave his neck for free. Pretty good deal, if you ask me.

I guess these were the compromises I had to make to insure that he wouldn't give up his apartment and move in lock, stock, and hideous works of art. He says, and I have to believe him, that he likes the arrangement the way it is—as he puts it, "a domestic lifestyle," with an escape hatch if he needs it.

A lot of people don't understand this arrangement. One ex-friend accused us of not having a "real" relationship. Fifteen years and we still can't make the type of commitment that most people consider the next logical step: either living together or . . . marriage. What's wrong with us? Other people seem to have no trouble with this living together thing. Even some of the most dysfunctional people seem to be able to cohabit for years and years. Exhibit A: Joey and Mary Jo Buttafuoco.

All right, maybe that's not a good example. But, many people who are completely unsuited to each other seem to be able to do it. Take my mother and father. They stayed married and living under the same roof for fifty years. Their differences were monumental. My mother was an opera freak. She could stand at that kitchen sink for hours listening to *La Bohème*, while my father was either at the track or lolling around on his beach chair in front of the OTB parlor. She was a slow eater, savoring each bite; he would be done with his meal before she could say, "You want some cheese on that?" No sooner had he finished eating, than he'd be out the door and we wouldn't see him again until late at night. That's when the nagging would start. "Where were you all night? Can't you remember to bring home a container of milk? Stop going through my pocketbook. Why did I marry you? Why was I born? Why am I living?"

My father would respond with a shrug or an answer that was a complete non sequitur. The question "Why can't you pick up your socks?" would be met with "Because the mon-

She loves him . . .

. . . she loves him not.

key died." He did have a wacky sense of humor, let's face it, but there was definitely a communication problem.

At home he said very little, except every once in a while he'd sort of grunt the word *salt* in the general direction of my mother. And there didn't have to be food anywhere in the vicinity when he said it. When my mother would nag him about his gambling, or about being out all night, he'd simply launch into his Calabrese mantra, *Chi muzzicadi i mini?!*, which means "Who's biting on your tits?!"

Merely uttering the word *bread* would elicit an immediate response from my mother that would rival a red alert at the war room in the Pentagon. A raised eyebrow would cause her to run to the refrigerator to make him a pepper and egg sandwich at any hour of the day or night. But, unlike Edith Bunker, who waited on Archie willingly, my mother waited on my father grudgingly. Bitching while sautéing was her raison d'être.

For years, I tried to figure them out. Why did they ever get married? My mother was no help at all in answering this question. Whenever I'd broach the subject, she didn't have an answer that made the slightest bit of sense. "Because I was stupid," was the best she could come up with. This, from a woman who was capable of completely rewiring a house if necessary. I never bothered to ask my father, but that's because to me it was obvious why he had married my mother. She was cute, she was fun, and he never had to lift a finger around the house.

They couldn't have always been like this or else he never

would have gotten her down the aisle. The story goes that while they were in their twenties, my father pursued my mother relentlessly. She would go out on a date with some guy in the neighborhood, and he would wait on her stoop until she got home. This must have put a slight damper on her dating opportunities. It so happens that Richard Nixon did the same thing to his wife Pat. He'd drop her off in L.A. somewhere, another guy would meet her and take her out on a date, and then, at the end of the date, Nixon would meet up with her and drive her home. Was Nixon a dog with a bone, superdependent, or just nuts? Maybe he was practicing techniques he would later use while hunting Communists with Senator Joe McCarthy. ("Are you now, or have you ever dated Pat Nixon?")

At any rate, what fascinates me is that here I am thinking that my father is some sort of underdeveloped Neanderthal, and instead he's on the same developmental level as one of the presidents of the United States, even if it was only Richard Nixon.

Eventually my father wore my mother down. Either that, or everyone else in the neighborhood was afraid to ask her for a date. But the question still remains: Why did they stay married? Was it, perhaps, a sexual attraction? Early on, I couldn't possibly fathom that this was the reason. What daughter thinks of her parents in flagrante delecto? Yet, my mother, even after years with him, dropped hints such as, "You know, your father enjoys his matinees." I never even saw them go to the movies together. What could she mean? All those afternoons, I thought she was upstairs listening to *La Traviata*, and those high notes apparently were not coming from the radio.

But if the sex was that good, why was she so miserable?

There was never any doubt that my father loved my mother and vice versa. And yet she always seemed on the verge of killing him.

There's only one thing that could turn an opera lover into a homicidal maniac. In addition to being in love with her, my father was also in love with gambling. He was obsessed with the ponies. One day I thought he was having a petit mal seizure, but it turned out that he was just listening to the race results at Belmont. This was the one thing about him that drove her over the edge. But it was not enough to divorce him. Today, a marriage will dissolve faster than you can say Larry King, but in those days, apparently it was considered life without parole. I personally thought they should have split up, especially at times when she seemed to be at the end of her rope. Once, as a married adult, I had a conversation with my mother that really left me more confused than ever. We were sitting in the kitchen one morning and she decided to talk.

Mother: Your father was out all night gambling again.

Me: What else is new?

Mother: He lost five hundred dollars last night. When I

think of all the money he's lost.

Me: You should have left him years ago.

Mother: At least he never hit me.

Me: That's true. He wasn't so bad.

Mother: He wasn't so bad? He lost fifty thousand dollars over the years.

Me: That son of a bitch gambled all that money?

Mother: Is that how you talk about your father?

Me: I'm sorry. I shouldn't call him names.

Mother: And why not? That rat bastard. We could have had a house. We could have gone out to dinner once in a while.

Me: What about a vacation? We never went anywhere, unless you count the cemetery.

Mother: Vacations are dangerous. Don't you remember when Vinnie Gargano drowned in Lake Hopatcong?

Me: That's why we never went on vacation? Because nobody in this neighborhood knows how to swim?

Mother: That and because your father gambled all the money he made. He was hooked on those stupid horses and card games.

Me: It's not just the gambling. You were his servant. All he had to do to get a beer was to grunt and you would jump.

Mother: Listen, your father worked hard all day and he got thirsty. There's one thing you women's libbies don't get. It's a woman's job to take care of her husband. They can't do it for themselves. You remember that and you'll always have a happy marriage.

Historically, women have been putting up with a lot of major and minor annoyances in order to maintain the institution of marriage (or a reasonable facsimile). My mother put up with my father's gambling obsession, Olga Koklova put up with Pablo Picasso's massive ego, Hillary Clinton puts up with Bill's indiscretions, and even Maria Shriver puts up with Arnold's annoying accent. Obviously there are compensations. For instance, Olga Koklova had the opportunity to get her face into the Museé Picasso in Paris (albeit a twisted face) and Hillary got to run the country without having to get elected, and as for Maria, heavy lifting is no longer an issue.

What I've learned about myself throughout a long marriage and a long relationship is that I have a very low tolerance for any annoyances. Living together, in or out of a marriage, only magnifies these little irritations that set my teeth on edge.

I now know that I could be living with St. Francis of Assisi and be irritated by his need to be good all the time. Still, I have to ask myself: Why can't I deal with loud chewing, heavy breathing, humming, tapping, or watching a husband just lying around the house with nothing to do? On the other hand, can't I just be in love with a guy and not have him around all the time? I guess I've been lucky with my current b.f. He seems to have as low a tolerance for having me around full time as I have for him (even though I can't imagine what irritating habits I could possibly have).

Random Thought

Living Will⌃

There's a movement afoot that I find especially unnerving. People who do not want to be resuscitated now have the option to wear a bracelet that says DO NOT RESUSCITATE. To me this sounds like a great gift for someone you hate. What if you put the wrong bracelet on one night? You're out having dinner, enjoying the company of friends, you feel faint. You pass out and twenty minutes later you're in the morgue. And all you wanted to do was accessorize.

Leni Riefenstahl: An Imaginary Interview

Leni Riefenstahl was the director and writer of *Triumph of the Will*, a propaganda film used by Hitler to advance Nazism. I watched a film biography of her recently. It traced her life in Germany in the thirties and forties to her present career as a cinematographer of life under the sea. There was something about her when she was interviewed that disturbed me greatly and I wanted to get a shot at her myself. Here is the interview I will never have with her.

Me: Leni, tell me about Nazi Germany during the war.
Leni: Oh, not that again. Nazis, Nazis. I'm sick to death of hearing that word. They've been hounding me for fifty years over this. I wasn't involved. I knew one Nazi during the war. One.

Me: Which Nazi was that?

Leni: Hitler. I knew him, but not when he was a Nazi. I knew him briefly when he was a house painter.

Me: Oh. What was he like then?

Leni: A very picky eater. That's all I remember. You give him a schnitzel, he's not happy. Just a big pain in the ass. Drove Eva Braun nuts all those years. The woman could never make him a meal that was for him satisfactory.

Me: Why did she stay with him if he was such a pain in the ass?

Leni: The battered wife syndrome. She suffered from it.

Me: He hit her?

Leni: Why not? He hit everyone else, didn't he? Then he would come crawling back begging for her forgiveness, whining like some sick schnauzer.

Me: Were you in Germany during the war?

Leni: Sure. Where would I be? I'm German.

Me: Didn't you realize what was going on?

Leni: What? What was going on?

Me: The Nazis were murdering people. Does the word *Treblinka* ring a bell?

Leni: Never heard of it. I didn't read the papers. Too depressing.

Me: Didn't you read *Mein Kampf*?

Leni: No. I heard it was boring. A big fat bore. Hitler was boring. All the time with the Jews. It was a repetition compulsion with Hitler. Boring, boring, boring.

Me: What about Kristallnacht?

Leni: I knew nothing about it. I was having my hair done in Dusseldorf that night. I was under the dryer. I heard nothing. I'm not interested in politics. Anyway, I was a filmmaker, an artist.

Me: You made *Triumph of the Will*, a movie about the glory of the Nazis. Don't you think that contributed to the Nazi effort?

Leni: One stupid movie and they never let me live it down. Nobody ever mentions my other movies where I was against the Nazis. Did you ever hear of *Take My Nazi, Please?*

Me: I don't think so.

Leni: Of course not. I couldn't get a distributor to save my life in Munich. That's because Hollywood is run by . . . (*her voice trails off.*)

Me: Run by who?

Leni: Whatever. Is this interview over yet? I'm starving for some Hoppel-Poppel.

Me: What are you doing now?

Leni: I do underwater cinematography.

Me: So. You're finally sleeping with the fishes.

Leni: That is some American expression that you used, *ja?*

Me: Bingo. And here's a Yiddish expression you might like: *Kish mir in tuches.**

*Kiss my ass.

Celebrity Sucking Up

It is a well-established fact that the best way to get celebrities to like you is to suck up to them, telling them how wonderful they are, how talented they are, how beautiful/handsome they are. So remember this litle piece of advice the next time you run into me (or vice versa).

Funny, fabulous, totally renovated.

Big star, never heard of him
before today, Garth Brooks.

How amazing could he be if he thinks we're dating? Kreakin, Joy, and Harvey Fierstein.

Great diet guru and foot
fetishist. Richard Simmons.

Vanessa Redgrave wearing a tallis. Who knew she was Jewish?

Dancing doggy-style with Burt Reynolds.

He could
have me if
he wanted.

He could
have me,
too, if he
wanted.

He had me.
Love that
tush.

The Wrong Century to Be a Woman

Publishers can come out with as many magazines as they want featuring women who are, as they like to put it, "big and fabulous and full-figured and sassy," but trust me, no woman wants to be fat. A man considers a date successful if he gets laid. A woman considers a date successful if she can stay on her diet during dinner.

Women will do almost anything to get thin and then stay thin. Every month, women's magazines are filled with diet tips that are virtually impossible to stick with. One woman wrote that she climbs thirty flights of stairs a day to take off the pounds. A realistic regime only if you work in the Empire State Building. Another woman shared the supposedly helpful information that she eats chicken with a melon baller to make it last longer. Could these tips be any more pathetic?

This obsession with thinness was not always the case.

When Rubens was a painter, it was an asset to be a plus size. Go over to the Metropolitan Museum some day and ask the guard at the door, "Where is the fat century?" They know exactly how to direct you. If you weighed over 175, you would be a model. Kate Moss would have been a checkout girl at the A&P. Roseanne? Miss Milan 1537. Can you imagine what the modeling schools were like back then?

"Buon giorno, and welcome to our orientation meeting at the Forgotten Ragazza of Firenze. I trust that you all ate the requisite anchovy pizza last night so that you will be retaining water for your first sitting. Remember the school's slogan: *'Mangia questa cotoletta o ti getto dalla finestra!'* (Eat this cutlet or I'll throw you out the window!).

"A word of warning: Last semester, some of the girls were seen jogging over by the Arno and were expelled. Let me be perfectly clear. There will be no physical exercise whatsoever during the school term. That includes stretching and reaching, except for a third helping of manicotti at the Medici buffets held daily.

"Needless to say, you are all to stay on the high cholesterol diet as recommended by the school nutritionist, Domenico DeLuisa. He recommends that 80 percent of your diet should come from saturated fat sources. Let's stop the insanity and start gorging.

"Now, about the artists. On the night before your sitting, I suggest an avocado mask which you can eat later, plus stopping by Il Castello Bianco (White Castle) for a gross of

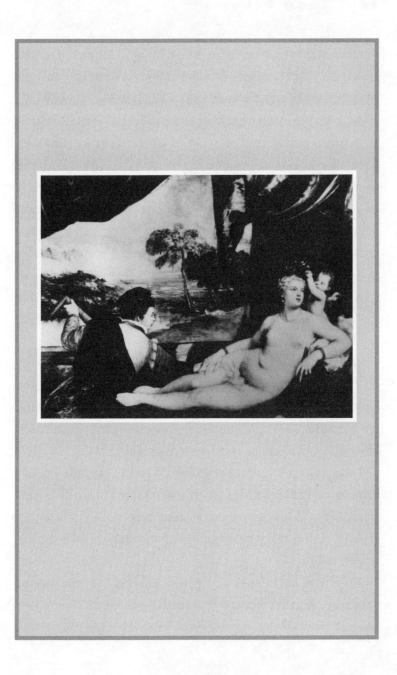

burgers. Remember, a svelte model is an unemployed model and will end up hemming skirts for Pope Leo at the Vatican.

"Let me say a few words about Titian whose latest work, *The Rape of Europa,* is winning prizes. The title is a misnomer as his impotency is known from Modena to Catania and back. Ask any *putana* on the Via Veneto. He's all talk. Even so, the bad news is that he's in denial and he will do anything to get into your pants, so don't lose a pound and there won't be any room for him. The good news is that he's a chubby chaser, so you girls will have a lot of work.

"Boycott Botticelli. His *Venus* was a huge hit and the word is out that his model is verging on anorexia at only 160. This trend toward thinness must be fought with everything we've got if we are to remain tops in our field.

"Rubens is a sneak. He may offer you a diet cappuccino to test your willpower. Don't fall for it. He's been burned in the past by yo-yo dieters. Last year some of his models dropped ten pounds over the summer by consuming low-fat biscotti and he'll go ballistic if this happens again."

I would have loved that century! What an attitude I could have had. "Whaddya mean, no dessert? I've got a sitting with Caravaggio in the morning! If that man doesn't see some cellulite, I'm history. Now gimme that cannoli, you chauvinist pig."

Alas, it is no longer the age of adipose, but the age of anorexia. And it's getting worse. Twenty years ago, a size twelve was considered small. Now, a size twelve sounds like a hippo size. Stores actually carry size zero! What adult woman wears a size zero? Do they want us to disappear altogether?

I, for one, can't fit into any of these clothes. They're too narrow. Why don't these stores stop wasting my time and name the department what it really is? Not Juniors. Not Misses. It's Anorexics and Bulimics. In fact, why not just have them call out the floor in the elevator: fifth floor: Eating Disorders. It would save all of us a lot of time.

In a recent issue of *Psychology Today*, women said they'd be willing to give up more than three years of their life to be their ideal weight. That's three years of bitching about being fat. Three years of cursing your genes. Three years of using a melon baller to eat your chicken! Gee, sounds like a good deal to me.

Some of the diets available to us are, let's face it, hideous. In one of them, you even have to weigh your meat. Talk about unnatural acts! Remember the case of Jean Harris, an otherwise intelligent woman—she was a teacher, actually—who shot and killed her lover, Dr. Herman Tarnower, the creator of the Scarsdale diet. In my opinion, he deserved it. Did you ever take a look at that diet? The man suggested that you take lamb chops to the office. This little tip goes way beyond sadism. No wonder she shot him. Who wouldn't?

A lot of so-called experts say that exercise is the key to losing and keeping off weight. And maybe it is. But not for those of us born prior to 1970. Our experience with exercise was limited to being forced to take gym classes for which you had to wear these hideous green bloomers with the elastic around the thigh that made you look like some 1890s bathing beauty with the fat pushed down to your legs. The only organized group activity we engaged in was volleyball, which required a fleet of twenty girls. Today, so many years after graduation, it's not so easy to, you'll excuse the expression, round up twenty willing and able women to play volleyball, especially after a manicure. Jogging has never been of much interest to the women in my generation. There isn't a sports bra made to counteract the continuous bouncing of the breasts in a well-endowed woman. Sure, if you're flat-chested, you can run or jump rope with abandon, but if your boobs are big enough to kick into that mammogram vise, then they're too big to bounce around in. They say that a girl over the age of fifteen should be able to do thirty-five sit-ups a day. I don't know about you, but I haven't done thirty-five sit-ups in my entire life. I'd rather wear black in August than do one sit-up.

As we age, it becomes harder and harder to lose weight. When I was in my twenties, I'd knock off a pound a day by eliminating bread or cake. The weight would just melt off. Now, if I lose two pounds a year, after practically starving myself, it's a source of celebration, which immediately puts six pounds back on. It doesn't matter what you give up. Believe me when I tell you I haven't looked at a pat of butter since

I saw *Last Tango In Paris*, but have I lost a single ounce? No.

This obsession to be thin causes women to be competitive with each other to the point of danger. Women who are self-conscious about their weight are a menace to other women. I have a friend who actually told me that she'd rather be dead than be fat. This is a woman who, if I order a sandwich at lunch, she'll order a salad. If I order a salad, she'll order half a cantaloupe. If I order half a cantaloupe, she'll order a cup of coffee. This bizarre contest continues until she's down to sucking on a mint-flavored toothpick. At this rate, her preference for dying over being fat could be a reality sooner than she thinks.

In the end, a word to the wise is sufficient. Statistically, skinny women die younger than fat women. Why? Because fat women are killing them.

Je Ne
Regrette Rien

One night, I was flipping through the TV channels and I happened to come across Catherine Deneuve being interviewed
by Charlie Rose. She looked as beautiful as ever in that ice
queen way that turns men into butter and women into lesbians.

Although she is a big film star in France, Americans
remember her more for her Chanel No. 5 commercials than
for her movies. I never understood what she was saying in
those ads. I would pull the TV closer to the bed, hoping I
could catch it. She'd say in that sexy French accent of hers
something like, "When you are a woman, you are glad,
because a man wants a woman to be a woman. But, you want
to be yourself. This makes me laugh. Ha! Ha! Ha! Ha!" She
sounded like she was reading from Sartre's *Being and
Nothingness*. I wanted to ask her, "What is the existential vac-

uum and does it come with attachments?" But, alas, she was in France, so I never got around to it.

Still, I could not keep my eyes off of her. In the movies she appears in, I always resent having to read subtitles because they take my gaze away from her face. Hedy Lamarr was beautiful. Lana Turner was beautiful. But neither of those actresses had what Deneuve had all her life: a French accent.

At one point in the interview, Charlie Rose asked Catherine Deneuve, "Do you have any regrets?" She paused, she stared, she pondered. Finally, she answered. "Of course I do. I have many regrets." And then she began to list them. Her husbands, her film roles, her face, her life. To my amazement, the woman was loaded with regrets.

This got me thinking about my Aunt Rose. Instead of turning men into butter, she turned ricotta into cheesecakes. A great cook, she was the Pavlov of Brooklyn, capable of causing involuntary salivating when she laid her hands on a piece of veal, turning pedestrian protein into delicious delicacies of Italian indulgence. Her life was spent cooking, reading cookbooks, and relating most conversations to her cooking. A typical interaction went like this:

> *Me:* I really think that feminists are becoming targets of some of these right-wing politicians who feel threatened by them.
>
> *Aunt Rose:* Tell me something, Joy. Do you think I put too much bread crumbs in these artichokes?

Aunt Rose was married for hundreds of years to Uncle Joe, a man who modeled himself after his idol, Benito Mussolini. Once during Thanksgiving dinner while discussing politics, the word *fascist* somehow slipped out of my mouth. Uncle Joe, who had been sitting there comatose from the tryptophan, suddenly erupted like Mt. Vesuvius, launching into an animated defense of his hero, and started quoting Benito. "Fortunately, the Italian people are not yet accustomed to eating several times a day," and, "Mankind is tired of liberty." Apparently, Uncle Joe thought these were the statements of a benevolent leader. In the midst of this tirade, much to our amazement, he reached into his pocket and pulled out a newspaper clipping that had to be fifty years old, praising the punctuality of the Italian trains and denying any connection between his beloved Benito and the hideous Adolf. ("That was all just a nasty rumor started by the communists," he insisted.) As the discussion became more heated, Aunt Rose finally got involved, saying, "Joe, do you want more salt on your stuffed mushrooms or what?"

Aunt Rose was always the dutiful wife, running home from her job as a seamstress to make sure dinner was on the table. Her idea of women's liberation was having him butter his own bread. Joe was a skilled cabinet maker, with an eye for detail, even though he suffered from severe myopia. But he never rose before noon, which made it difficult to earn a decent living. Nevertheless, he always found time to go bowling, even into his late eighties, which earned him more

Uncle Joe?

grotesque trophies than could fit in their three-room, un-air-conditioned, plastic-covered apartment.

Aunt Rose was not a risk taker. Her idea of taking a chance was buying a domestic brand of tomato paste. Her fears concerning traveling, in particular, were ingrained. She would not go on a boat because "it could tip over" (she was not a lightweight, so perhaps this fear was justified), she never flew in a plane, and even an elevator seemed an ominous form of transportation in her mind.

Both she and Uncle Joe were born in Italy, but never, in their fifty-year marriage, did they go back to visit their roots. There was no interest on her part at all. I once asked her why she never went back and she replied, "Why should I? Everyone I knew there moved here." And Uncle Joe, even though he would have reveled in visiting the Victor Emanuel monument erected during Mussolini's reign, was too dependent on her home-cooked lasagne to chance leaving the neighborhood.

For all his bravado, Joe never mastered the English language and was always three steps behind in any conversation. He constantly complained to me and other relatives that we were talking too fast and about too many things all at once. His deficiencies with the language, along with his paltry income, did not deter him from being one of the most critical people I ever knew. Nothing impressed him. I graduated from college. Not good enough. I became a teacher. I should have become a dentist. When I was on television for the first time, all he could say was, "They made a fool out of you," a reference to the fact that part of my act was preempted.

In the great tradition of the apple doesn't fall far from the tree, his mother, who lived with Joe and Rose, was the Joan Crawford of the tenement building. Topping off at four feet, nine inches, and not speaking a word of English, she could start the War of Aunt Rose's with a lie, or a report to her son of alleged neglect by her daughter-in-law. Her mouth was foul and her mind so devious that often my aunt would find herself out of control with rage. One day, Aunt Rose couldn't take it anymore and washed her mother-in-law's mouth out with brown soap, the kind used on poison ivy. When Uncle Joe returned home from his three-hour workday, his mother's face was swollen like a zeppole from hell. Aunt Rose and Uncle Joe didn't speak for weeks after that and my aunt came and lived with me and my parents for a while. They eventually made up and for the rest of their lives, she defended him to anyone who dared to cast disparaging remarks his way, no matter how argumentative and vitriolic he got.

They were suited to each other, since Aunt Rose was never one to bestow a compliment when a barb would do just as well. My desire to lose weight has always haunted me, and she once counseled me on the subject: "Oh, you don't wanna lose too much weight. You'll be all teeth and mouth."

You might be wondering what all this has to do with Catherine Deneuve's interview on "The Charlie Rose Show."

Aunt Roʌe aʌ the young Edith Piaf.

Well, that interview made me recall a conversation I once had with Aunt Rose about her life. In fact, I asked her the very same question that Charlie asked Catherine: "Aunt Rose, looking back on your ninety-two-year life, do you have any regrets?" Without missing a beat, Aunt Rose said, "No. I wouldn't have done anything different at all." "Really?" I remember asking. "Nothing?" "Nothing," she answered, as she tasted the minestrone she was cooking.

So what can we learn from all this? That if you are adored by people all over the world, have had affairs and children with Marcello Mastroianni and Roger Vadim, if your profile is the model for the symbol of France, and everyone wants to sleep with you, *and* you have perfumes named after you and you are a size four, then you will have regrets. . .

But, if you lived in a tenement without air conditioning, never went anywhere or did anything, were married to a fascist who carried pictures of Mussolini in his wallet, and your favorite outfit was an apron over a sweater, then you will have no regrets.

And what of Edith Piaf, the famous French chanteuse, whose famous line is *Je ne regrette rien*? (I regret nothing.)

Do you think maybe she also lived in a tenement with a fascist?

Random Thought

St. Patrick's Day Parade

Gays are not allowed to march in the St. Patrick's Day Parade in New York City, but someone from the Irish Republican Army did march. Now I ask you, who is more dangerous? A group who has been known to blow up buses, or people who know all the lyrics to Stephen Sondheim musicals?

Some Thoughts on the History of Birth Control, or PMS Flashbacks

I recently had occasion to look into the history of birth control and I found some pretty staggering information. Apparently, men and women have been trying for some time to come up with an effective method of birth control with very little success. And some of these methods have been pretty kinky. I thought I'd share some of them with you.

Prehistoric men basically believed in magic and they were quite sexist. They thought that the male contained all the elements of reproduction and the female was just the incubator. The fact that a lot of the babies looked exactly like their mothers didn't seem to bother them at all, as they were too busy worshiping their sperm.

Once prehistoric man figured out that women had something to do with conception, they had to come up with ways to control it. The early Egyptians came up with the first spermicide: crocodile dung. This was not a thrilling method, especially if you wanted a date, so Cleopatra figured a way to circumvent this. Since she only had three children (one with Julius Caesar and two with Mark Antony), she must have known what she was doing. Cleo used olive oil to cover her cervix. Not only did she prevent conception, but the first Caesar salad was born.

During the Middle Ages, a regression took place and even Albert the Great, one of the most learned men of his age, was stumped. The only thing he could come up with was that if a woman didn't want to conceive, she should eat some bees and spit thrice into the mouth of a frog. Many women not only got pregnant using this technique, but there was a hideous outbreak of mouth warts.

The chastity belt was used on women when their husbands had to go to war during the Crusades. It's a common misconception (no pun intended) that the best job in those days was knight of the round table. Not true. The best job was to be a locksmith.

Various attempts by other cultures at birth control were also unsuccessful. The famous Middle Eastern physician Ali Ibn Abba suggested the insertion of rock salt. Now, that has got to hurt, and it did nothing to prevent births, but the traffic in Persia did run smoothly.

Avicenna, a renowned physician of Islam, recommended violent backward jumping after sex. Kind of a dyslexic bunny hop. Surprise. Didn't work.

St. Paul, an early adherent of the Nancy Reagan school of abstinence, told women to "just say no." Did it work? What do you think?

The Mexican Indian women ate tons of yams. Not only didn't this work, but the babies were all born orange and had very tough skin.

Ismail Jujani suggested that simultaneous orgasm be avoided. Most women's reaction: Hey, no problem.

Hippocrates noted that fat women tended to be infertile and he advocated weight gain. Bring on the Ben and Jerry's.

Things started to pick up around the eighteenth century, with Casanova. He was the first man to dream up a sort of cervical cap. He used a half lemon, which was a fairly effective early barrier method. It also made a great margarita to get a woman in the mood.

Two devices that were eventually developed and had a high degree of efficacy were the diaphragm and the IUD. The beauty of these gadgets is that they make nice accessories when they're no longer used for birth control. See next page.

The rhythm method was used early on and women would have to regulate themselves by the phases of the moon. Not so easy on a cloudy night or if you are nearsighted or blind.

Soranos suggested inserting pulverized pomegranate or

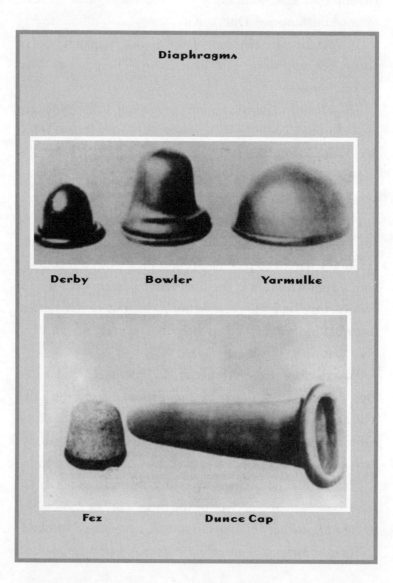

Diaphragms

Derby   Bowler   Yarmulke

Fez   Dunce Cap

the pulp of dried figs into the vagina. I wonder if there is any data on the correlation between years of famine and increased birth rates due to the fact that no one could get their hands on all this food that women were stuffing into their birth canals.

The condom is still effective, especially these days. There is a new female condom out, but you need a shoe tree to put it in. It's made by Hefty. The cable guy installs it (between 9 and 11 A.M.). The male condom comes with instructions that include the words *be sure to put on before penetration.* Listen, if you know a guy who can put it on after penetration, would you give him my number?

Random Thought

Give the DNA a Chance to Breathe

The trouble with the monarchy of England is that there is too much inbreeding. For centuries they've been marrying within royal blood lines and as a result, they've produced some really stupid heirs.

Take the case of King Edward VIII, who abdicated the throne back in the thirties in order to marry an American woman named Wallis Simpson. No beauty, she must have done something really, really good (the men know what I mean). Anyway, I suspect he was one brain cell away from a bowl of oatmeal. In his letters, published recently, he writes to her, and I quote: "Dear

Wally, I hope a girl is missing a boy, because a boy is missing a girl, and hopes that a girl loves a boy because a boy loves a girl." And then he signs the letter, "Well, I have to make drowsy now." THIS IS THE FUTURE KING OF ENGLAND. Thank goodness he abdicated because he was going to have to deal politically with his friend Adolf Hitler. Can you imagine that correspondence? "Dear Adolf, I hope a boy is not thinking of invading Poland. Well, I have to make drowsy now."

Perhaps the royal family should consider introducing mixed marriages into the fold (i.e., an Italo-Hebraic combo platter or a black and a white to produce a stunning little mocha child). It could save them in the end.

Camille
and Gloria

I don't want to drop names, but I am friends with both Gloria Steinem, one of the founders of the modern women's movement, and Camille Paglia, a self-proclaimed "antifeminist feminist." Camille has been quite clear about her disdain for Gloria and other traditional feminists. Having heard some of Camille's diatribes against her, I can't imagine that Gloria has Camille on her Christmas card list.

I admire both of them and I think that they could be friends if only they sat down, face to face, and hashed out their differences (a few martinis couldn't hurt either). The chances of that happening, however, seem to be equal to Charlton Heston donating his toupee to a bald liberal. I don't think I could even get them into the same room, so my fantasy life has driven me to come up with the conversation that I'm missing. Of course, my presence could be a stabilizing influence. I imagine the following conversation:

Joy: Gloria, why don't you start?

GS: Camille, don't you think that calling for my assassination was a bit over the top?

CP: You're a menace. You've ruined the feminist movement. Your thinking has not evolved since the day you discovered a brassiere was extraneous. And because of your sniveling obsession with victimization, we're all running around so uptight that men can't even look at us. I can't even make a joke about a guy's dick at the water cooler anymore because of you, okay. You've driven us into the magma flow of the Earth's crust with your whiny, nasal ranting and I'm sick of it. Women are tough and we don't need to be victims anymore, okay. Everything about your movement is dead.

GS: The only one who feels victimized is me. By you. And might I add, Miss Opportunist, that you walked into the women's movement with your own agenda, figuring that this is the way to make your mark. On my back and on the backs of all the women who have suffered at the hands of sexist pigs all these years.

CP: See? That's what I mean. Suffered. Suffered. Suffered. Okay. Suffered.

Joy: Camille, can I ask you a personal question? Do you have Tourette's syndrome?

CP: No, I don't. St. Rocco, one of the great saints, the saint of hopeless causes, a man with an advanced zeitgeist, had Tourette's syndrome. I suppose, Miss Injured Party, you'd say that St. Rocco is a victim also?

GS: Even with saints, you identify with men. What is it with you? Did you want to be a boy? Is that it? Did your mother really want a boy, Camille? Or are you the kind of girl who always wanted all the boys to like you so you turned your back on the girls? It's pathetic to listen to your neediness for male identification and attention.

CP: After a quarter century of male bashing, you have the *cojones* to tell me that I identify with men and that that is a bad thing? Somebody has to stand up against the vicious attacks from the so-called feminists. You and your bourgeois fantasies have infantilized even the most macho of men. Thank god you didn't live during the Napoleonic era, or we would have to be looking at pictures of him with his hand on his balls instead of in his jacket. As I say in my book *Vamps and Tramps*, women of your ilk will cause the penis to shrink into the next millennium with your weaselly vaginal rhetoric.

GS: Why do you blame the computer for the floppy disk?

Joy: Huh?

CP: Listen, you pillar of weltschmerz. As I said in my first book, *Sexual Personae* . . .

GS: Do you only quote from your own books?

CP: As I was saying, the issue is that if Michelangelo were Michelangela, there would be no *David*, okay. Because women do not possess the necessary testosterone factors to produce a work of art, okay. If it were left to women like you, if women in sixteenth-century Italy were like you, there would be no Pieta, okay. There would be no Sistine Chapel, okay. There would just be a bunch of beauty parlors.

GS: Now you've gone too far. My sisters and I have been fighting against lookism since the beginning of the women's movement.

CP: Maybe you should have given Betty Friedan a makeover.

GS: Listen, you man junkie, leave Betty out of this. The woman changed the face of feminism. She didn't need to change her own face.

CP: Oh, as if looks mean nothing. Give me a break, okay. I wasn't the one who worked at the Playboy Club dressed up as a bunny and flaunting myself all over the place.

GS: That, for your information, was for investigative reporting. Sure, I made a couple of bucks in tips, but I blew the whistle on Hugh Hefner, who made his living from the exploitation and objectification of women who still to this day only make seventy-four cents to every dollar that your precious boys make.

CP: Hugh Hefner is a saint. His zeitgeist is not as big as St. Rocco's but he is a saint. His so-called objectification liberated women to the status of goddess. If you knew anything about liberation, you would see that men who read *Playboy* grovel at the feet of women.

Joy: That's so they can look up their dresses.

GS: Your distortion of reality is mind-boggling. How are six-inch heels, a push-up bra and bunny ears liberating? Who did you study with, RuPaul?

CP: Your condescension toward women is apparent in your lack of a coherent thought process. In prehistoric Africa, clothing was instituted not for bad weather, since the temperatures rose to 150 Fahrenheit on a good day. No. Clothing was worn by women as decoration, to lure the men into the cave. It was power through the loincloth. Bunnies had that same power over the troglodytes who frequented the Playboy Clubs. You're such a whiny troll yourself that you don't see that. All you see is exploitation and vexation.

GS: Who are you calling a whiny troll, you hyperactive overmotorized Chihuahua.

CP: Who are you calling a Chihuahua, you four-eyed anorexic?

Joy: You know, Gloria, that's a cute top you're wearing. Where did you get it?

GS: Loehmann's.

CP: I love that place. Their philosophy is so like the Greek *agora* concept. Plato himself correlated his allegory of the cave to women's propensity for bartering during the Hellenic age.

GS: (*wistfully*)My mother and I used to shop at Loehmann's when I was young and still fertile.

CP: (*tearfully*)You're having a Proustian moment, Gloria, and that top is definitely your color.

GS: You think so?

CP: (*starting to cry*) You're a winter, I think.

GS: And you're an autumn, aren't you?

CP: (*blubbering*) Yes I am. No one ever noticed it before.

GS: Camille, isn't it wonderful? You're not hiding behind your rage anymore. The real Camille is emerging. Tell us about the hurt you had in childhood. Was it horrible for you? Share with us. The patriarchy victimized us all.

CP: Oh, no you don't. I'm not falling for that. I'm not getting sucked into this moribund fin de siècle version of feminism.

Joy: All right, I gave it a shot. Let's shop!

Random Thought

Doctors and Their Big Mouths

When I was growing up, doctors were different from the way they are today. For one thing, they made house calls. For another thing, they didn't feel compelled to tell you that you had six months to live.

Today, they lie about everything else, but when you're about to be fixed up with the grim reaper they feel this is something they have to tell you. Who needs this information? Doctors should be a little selective about who they tell. Go tell Shirley MacLaine that she has a week to live. She doesn't care; she's coming back. Go tell Pat Buchanan. Maybe it'll keep him from running for office. But a neurotic agnostic from Brooklyn you don't tell. This information is not going to help me, because a neurotic agnostic from Brooklyn is not going to go gracefully and quietly. No. She's going to suck the life out of everyone around her. Friends, relatives, and especially the moronic doctor who told her.

The Incredible, Absolutely True Story of Lorena and John

By now the story of Lorena and John Wayne Bobbit is legendary. But few among us know the true story of how the phrase "to bobbitize" became part of the English language. Here then is the absolutely, positively, true-life tale of the tragic love story that captivated America and put the fear of God into philandering men . . . at least for a while.

Like all married couples, Lorena and John Wayne Bobbit, named after that famous kickass movie star of those old westerns, whose real name, by the way, was Marion, had their ups and downs. The downs usually came as a result of John's nasty habit of beating his wife.

One day, Lorena, or Lo as she was sometimes called, decided she couldn't take it anymore. She knew she had to do something, but she didn't know what. One very hot evening, while pondering her options—she could always leave the cad—Lo found herself with a powerful thirst, so she went into the kitchen to get a glass of water. While she was standing in front of the kitchen sink, she said to herself, You know, I'm really not that thirsty, after all. What I really feel like doing is . . . cutting off his penis . . .

So she picked up a big, very big, sharp, very sharp knife and went into the bedroom and, while he was lying there fast asleep, she sliced off her husband's penis, just like that. And then, because she was a very good housekeeper and didn't want to leave a mess, she picked it up, went outside, and threw it into the woods.

Now that might be the end of the story, but it wasn't. In fact, this is where it really gets interesting. Because as soon as John Wayne Bobbit woke up and realized that something very important of his was missing, he called the police. And since it was obviously a slow night, and the police had little else to keep themselves occupied, they found that missing penis in only two hours. Can you believe it? Just two measly hours. That, my friends, is an example of excellent police work. After all, these same policemen have been looking for Jimmy Hoffa's entire body for twenty years now, and they haven't located a damn thing.

And Amelia Earhart? Not a trace. And yet this little pig in the blanket they were able to find in two hours.

Of course, you have to remember that it was men who were looking for this appendage, not women. And, after all, they are very familiar with that particular piece of equipment they were looking for. And why shouldn't they be? They're always touching it. Admiring it. Constantly comparing and measuring it. And so, the fact is, a blind man could probably have found it, no matter how deep into the woods she might have thrown it.

And it's a very good thing they did find it. Because if they hadn't even today, years after Lorena took the law into her own hands, we'd probably still be looking at that little thing on milk cartons.

Sadie.

Sadie's News and Advice from the Neighborhood

Growing up in Brooklyn in the forties and fifties, not everyone had a television and so much of the news, especially of the local variety, traveled by mouth rather than over the airwaves. In every neighborhood there was always someone who seemed to be the local version of Dan Rather, the town crier, and the *National Enquirer* all rolled up into one. For us, it was Sadie, and here's a sample of the kinds of neighborhood tidbits she disseminated.

1. Former bodyguard Carmine Russo has become a faith healer. There isn't a cripple left in the neighborhood since Carmine has been pronouncing his miraculous words: Walk or I'll break both your legs.

2. Attention dog lovers. Tragedy struck the home of Maria Fantasia this week when her hundred-pound cocker spaniel exploded in her kitchenette after eating an entire tray of lasagna. A shocked neighbor was quoted as saying, "That dog never moved. I thought it was a statue."

3. Frances Calabrese had a dream. That someday her son, Frankie, would receive his diploma from a legitimate medical school and become a doctor. Well, her dream did not come true. Frankie is now headlining at the Club Safari in Newark, New Jersey, as a female impersonator. "I still want to be a doctor," said Frankie, applying his mascara, "but, do you know how hard it is for a woman to get into medical school?" So much for a mother's heartbreak.

4. Only a hail of bullets marred the festivities as wedding bells rang for Concetta Rose Caratucci and Angelo J. Balducci Jr. in Our Lady of the Most Precious Blood Church. Angelo J. Balducci Sr. is the brother of the late Cici "The Rat" Balducci, owner of the Sacred Heart Macaroni Co. Anthony, Ralphie boy, and Nando "Go Fish" Balducci, brothers of the groom, took cover in a nearby pew as they pulled the senior Balducci down with them. The bride is a graduate of the Mr. Dominick's School of Beauty Culture and a member of the Young Hoods Cultural Club. She was a vision in a hundred yards of silk organza chiffon designed by Creations de Felice of Astoria. After a two-and-a-half-day honeymoon in the Poconos, the happy couple will reside in

an undisclosed two-family brick somewhere in the Bronx. My lips are sealed.

5. Will success spoil Tony Gozzicalado? What with his new hit CD, *She's Cheap, but She's Beautiful,* selling nearly fifty copies, we may be losing him to Hollywood. If Tony's wife, Lucia, has her way, Tony will stay right here on the block. "I don't care how big he gets," she is quoted as saying, "as long as he keeps his job in the bread store." Will Lucia let Tony be another Al Martino? Or is she gonna make him bust?

6. Vito Abonzette, judge of this year's Miss Italian American beauty contest, has announced that this year's winner is none other than Gloria Abonzette. Now I find this hard to digest, and all I can say is, There are none so blind as those who will not see.

7. We have a winner of the vegetable garden contest. I'm happy to announce that Cosmo Bruzzomato is the winner of this year's contest for having the biggest googootz in the neighborhood. His smiling wife was quoted as saying, "and they say that size don't matter."

8. Atheists, take note. Another miracle has taken place on Mulberry Street. Philomena Senzagoola reported that a vision appeared to her with a message. These are Philomena's exact words: "I was rinsing out a few things, when Our Lady appeared on top of my refrigerator. She looked so beautiful. Just like in her statues. I said to her, 'Get off the refrigerator. Have a cup of coffee.' And she said, 'No, my child. I'm in a

rush. But I wanted to come unto you to speak unto you these words: Don't make a scene at your sister Millie's wedding. And, short shorts are not for everybody.'"

And they say that God is dead.

Sadie took her responsibilities as a "newswoman" quite seriously, and so she also sometimes assumed the role of Ann Landers for those who had problems so serious that they had nowhere else to turn. Following are a few examples of Sadie's unrivaled wisdom.

Dear Sadie,

How do you keep your breasts so firm?

Signed,
Sagging on the Vine

Dear Sagging,

Most women lose the elasticity of their bosoms when they breastfeed. For those of you who are not as genetically blessed as I am, Niagara starch sprayed twice daily on to the nipples will do the trick.

Dear Sadie,

For our second honeymoon, my husband is taking me to Bermuda on the *Oceanic* liner. In preparation for the trip, do you think I should rent the Al Pacino movie *Cruisin'*?

Signed,
All at Sea

Dear All,

Don't let the title fool you. I once thought that the movie *Deep Throat* was the life story of Luciano Pavarotti.

Dear Sadie,

My daughter is getting married at Leonard's of Great Neck. Should I wear a hat over my new bouffant hairdo?

Signed,
Up in the Air with My Hair

Dear Up,

I suggest that you carry the hat. That way the public can feast upon both your hair and your hat. Also, wear sunglasses so that no one will recognize you.

Dear Sadie,

My husband is very touchy, but he's far from perfect. How can I tell him the truth without killing him?

Signed,
Perplexed on Ave. Z

Dear Perplexed,

Here's my secret. I practice what I call CHWOS. Criticize Humanely Without Severity. For example, let's say that you think your husband has a noxious odor to him. Don't say, as my sister Anna once said to her husband, *"Madonna, ce na puzza ca,"* which means, "Boy, does it stink here." Be tactful and say, "You know, this humidity really allows bacteria to grow rampant, don't you think?" Then, add a helpful hint to the discussion, such as, "A little Lysol under the armpit with your morning coffee will make you a new man."

Confidential to P.G.: Follow this tip and your husband's pizza business will pick up considerably, especially when he throws those pies up in the air.

How to Tell If You're Really Italian: The True and False Test

It has come to my attention that for some reason there is a small group of people who claim to be Italian even though they're not. In order to ascertain just who are the real Italians, I have devised a fool-proof true-false test. Take it, if you dare.

Give yourself one point for each correct answer.

1. *True or False:* A braciola is a lethal weapon.

2. *True or False:* A pitsuda is a Japanese motel.

3. *True or False:* If you had ten cannoli and eighteen sfogliatelli and you ate three pastaciotti after swallowing a pound of mortadella, you could be hungry at ten o'clock for a little dish of meatballs, or maybe a nice pepper and egg sandwich.

4. *True or False:* A rolling propetta gathers no sauce.

5. *True or False:* Figlia Bedda is a silent screen star.

6. *True or False:* Cuoricedda di Papa is a recent acquisition of the Metropolitan Museum of Art.

7. *True or False:* A sensible breakfast for an infant is pureed sausage and peppers.

8. *True or False:* Chi Fa is the brother of Kung Fu.

9. *True or False:* "People who live in glass houses should dress in the cellar" was said by Immanuel Kant.

Answers: 1. T; 2. F; 3. T; 4. T; 5. F; 6. F; 7. T; 8. F; 9. F

If you scored nine, you are definitely Italian. Go inside and take the plastic seat covers off the couch.

If you scored five to eight, you are eating at too many Italian restaurants and you're too involved in Tony Danza's career.

If you scored zero to four, fuhgedaboudit.